CW01023504

Sadie
The Little Farm Dog

Jane Smith

Jane Smith

ISBN: 978-0-9573505-4-0

JS Books WV6 7UE

CONTENTS

ACKNOWLEDGMENTS

PROOF READERS
Thanks are due to the proof readers, Ann Bickley, Jocelyn Lenham & Sandra Barber.

ILLUSTRATORS
The front cover illustration and all the interior illustrations are the work of Jeff Flanc. Brought up in Surrey, Jeff graduated in Fine Art from London Metropolitan University. He lives and works in London as an artist and illustrator.

The drawing on the back cover is by Flora Farrell. Flora is a Shropshire artist specialising in pet portraits and works under the name 'Flora and Fauna.'

1

INTRODUCTION

A good sheepdog is worth its weight in gold

During our time at the farm we had many collies. Even with a small flock of a hundred ewes a good sheepdog makes life so much easier than trying to do the job oneself. Too many hot days had been spent running up and down steep hills to move a flock in a certain direction, only for them to suddenly turn back, get their heads down again, and start to graze. Try gathering sheep into a pen when the grass in the field is lush and quite enough for their needs, thank you very much, and you will soon see how difficult sheep can be to move. Frustration sets in, and the lesson one learns pretty quickly is that a dog could do the job much better. There are two provisos; firstly that the man/woman knows how and secondly that the dog wants to work, not all dogs do.

It was July when we lost Jess our border collie. Postman Pat's cat was responsible for the name, no doubt, and needless to say, Jess was a beautiful black and white dog. She had been born on a farm and sold to a town home. We acquired her when she was six months old, very overweight, and with a distinctly doggy odour about her from too many hours spent in a kennel. It seemed that Jess's walks had consisted mainly of going to and from the chip shop, and her weight was testimony as to how much she enjoyed the cuisine. Jess was the perfect family pet but as far as sheep were concerned she didn't want to know. No matter what we tried she simply wasn't interested and would run home at the first opportunity. Perhaps she had had an unfortunate early experience on the farm where she was born, who knows, but my husband fell in love with the dog, and there would be no other collie on our farm as long as we had Jess. This meant that the family would just have to rally round and do the work for our reluctant sheepdog while she reclined on the sofa.

As always when one loses a dog there is the question of how quickly one can bear to replace it, or if one can bear to replace it at all. Eventually, and reluctantly, my husband agreed that we could have a new dog but then did nothing about it. The meaning of this was quite clear. If my husband had his way, there would be no new dog. Jess had been his best friend and he just couldn't get over the heartache of losing her; the idea of a replacement was unthinkable.

On the other hand, both myself and the children wanted another dog and it would be nice if it was a dog which would do some work. The question was how to resolve the dilemma of choosing a dog which would fit in. A puppy would require a lot of training but an older dog might have too many bad habits. We had usually acquired our dogs at around six months of age when the lovely little ball of fluff someone had bought at eight weeks old became a dog that needed both its brain and body exercising. Those who got rid of their dogs at this age did them a favour in rehoming them to our farm. We were definitely a soft touch. Yes, there were issues to be resolved, but generally they could be resolved or got round. Unfortunately, scan the papers as I might, there were no collies of that age being advertised. I put the word out but drew a blank. At this point someone suggested the local Border Collie Rescue group. I rang them up and explained what we were looking for. No, they had nothing at present, but would bear us in mind. Months went by and I thought we had been forgotten until one day the rescue group rang up and offered a male, black collie. I didn't think that would do at all. We had always had bitches before so I thought my husband might not take to a dog, and a black one at that. Fortunately the Rescue Centre said they had another couple interested in the dog so I let it go.

Autumn had turned into winter and it was February before I had another phone call. This time it was about a seven month old sheepdog bitch which had been picked up in Montgomery and taken to the Pound. The dog had been found running loose and on the two previous occasions when she had been impounded the family were allowed to have her back. On the third occasion I was told, the animal must be destroyed or re-homed. At this point Samaritans such as the Border Collie Rescue are notified and they must collect these dogs immediately or they will be put down. The downside of taking a dog from any rescue situation is that they come with baggage. Some have less than others but all have their suitcases.

With Jess, there were two issues; there was a total unwillingness to work, and a tendency to bite if you got too close to her. In this case I had an idea. Knowing the previous owner I could imagine how this might have happened. I asked him how he reprimanded the dog when she did something wrong. His reply was immediate,' I would call her to me and then tap her on the nose with a rolled-up newspaper.' Ah, yes, that would make any dog very wary about being too close to people, obeying the kindly call to come, and then on doing so being rewarded with a hefty whack on the nose. It might even explain her unwillingness to work. There was certainly a residual fear of certain people, evident one day when a man wearing a woollen hat was walking towards us along a narrow pavement. Jess was good on a lead so I wasn't ready for her reaction; she flew across the road, the lead coming straight out of my hand. Luckily someone caught her and it was a miracle that there wasn't a car passing. I never understood why that happened and I never saw that panic again.

Unravelling the 'whys,' and trying to resolve them, is particularly difficult when you have no idea of the background of the dog except that they were caught on the run. Anyway, this much we didn't think about when we had another phone call to say that we could visit the dog at a nearby kennels. Before we went, we had to be vetted to assess our suitability as owners. There were few questions in fact. We would have to have a home visit, but for now they would run through a checklist. The only question I remember was where the dog would live - in the house or in a kennel? I remember this because I thought what a daft question. A kennel is a perfectly acceptable home for a dog and some dogs simply refuse to sleep in a house, much preferring their own company and a view of the outdoors denied them within four walls. My answer reflected that opinion. 'She will live where she wants to live. If she prefers the house, then she is very welcome to sleep in it, otherwise she can have a kennel.' In the event, there was no home visit. Either the rescue centre was desperate to get rid of this dog to any 'sucker' who would have her, or we passed the test.

The day came when we were to visit our possible new dog and the news had to be delivered to my husband. This was the moment I was dreading. Any change was fiercely resisted and became a battle ground which I never learned how to deal with. Talking would have been my approach but it certainly wasn't my husband's. 'I think we need to talk about this,' was a phrase that was never heard in our house. So while I wasn't afraid of taking responsibility, I was very afraid of the consequences of so doing. My strategy was to delay telling Simon what I was going to do until the last possible moment, and then to run (sometimes literally) before the proverbial hit the fan. It was a strategy of delayed pain, but the inevitability of the repercussions built a fear in me until the moment when I had to face the music. The volume control only had two settings, at either end of the spectrum, and it was hard to know which was worse.

It was time to brace myself and reveal that we were going to look at a collie. The response was brief and predictable, 'I told you I didn't want another dog'. This increased my fear of the response when we did, eventually, return with a dog. Our experience with Jess was that once Simon got to know a new dog he would love her, but would that be so in this case? We could only hope for the best.

Arriving at the kennels we were taken to see our potential new family member. To say it was a shock isn't putting it too strongly. Over the years we had had dogs of various colours and sizes, brown and white, black and white and tricolour but they all had one thing in common; they looked like collies or sheepdogs of one sort or another. I had never seen a collie like this, a sheepdog of some sort, certainly, but who knew what. She was far too small, tiny in fact, a merle, a colour most sensible people will tell you to avoid, and most noticeably to me, her head was small and narrow. Perhaps, you may be thinking, what she didn't have in looks she made up for in her loving personality, but sadly not. She wasn't aggressive, which was a big plus, but she certainly wasn't overjoyed to see us. In fact, she simply ignored us, we didn't seem to feature in her world view at all. The question we should have been asking was how this dog would bond with any owner, but of course the obvious question is the one you don't ask. It's fair to say that we had many misgivings, so I have no idea why it was that when we were asked for a decision, I looked at my son, and for some unknown reason said, 'she's lovely, we'll have her.'

2

COMING HOME

We soon found out just how much Sadie liked her freedom

As we drove home, Sadie was not unduly excited or worried. She bounced around the back seat of the car a little but no more. It was a different matter when she went into the house. She raced into the kitchen and promptly jumped on the table. I had never seen anything like it. My husband came to see the new arrival and was distinctly unimpressed. He took one look at her and said simply, 'wasn't there any choice,' before going back into the sitting room and shutting the door firmly behind him. I could share his disappointment in many ways. She just wasn't what he had expected, either in looks or behaviour. I remember saying to a friend, 'but don't you think she is pretty?' 'No,' she said honestly, 'far too fox-like for my taste.'

I began to serve our evening meal - steak and kidney pie, I remember. Sadie had already been offered her meal but she seemed not to recognise either a dog's bowl or the food in it and walked away. I assumed that she would need to settle before she ate, but as I bent down to get the pie out of the oven there she was, quick as a flash, taking a large chunk of pie. I gripped the dish tightly or Sadie would have had the lot. How she didn't burn herself I will never know. We ate our meal in silence with me holding Sadie's collar very firmly to avoid her jumping on the table again and devouring the food from everyone's plates. When I eventually sat down in the sitting room exhausted, in she bounded and sat on my head. She was fast, unpredictable, and clearly had had no training whatsoever. The lack of aggression which had seemed such a positive, was far outweighed by this crazy behaviour. I went to bed that night thinking - 'what had we got,' and knowing that my husband would be thinking, 'I told you so, it's your problem'

The next day was even worse. Work had to carry on and Sadie had to stay indoors until she was familiar with her new surroundings. We put her in the garage and all went well until a friend came to visit. He had no idea we had a new dog and before I could say, 'don't open the door,' the deed was done, and out raced Sadie, up the drive and across a main road. I had never seen a dog run so fast. I ran in panic as this was such a busy road. I was angry, not that the friend had released the dog, but in his casual attitude. 'She'll be fine,' he said, as he sauntered up the drive. I had my doubts. The chances of her not being completely flattened on this road were pretty small. There was no screeching of brakes so we presumed she had reached the other side safely. Sure enough, there she was in a huge field, doing circuits at a speed which would have been impressive on a greyhound track. How to get her back was the problem since the field was unfenced. We called her to us and there was almost no response. Occasionally she would stop, look at us as though she might deign to return, and then carried on. Suddenly, with no apparent intention of coming back, she ran towards us, and just as we thought we might catch her, she swerved unexpectedly and raced back across the road in the direction of home. We followed despondently across the road and down the drive. Sadie was now exploring our fields in a similar, albeit less manic, way. When eventually we did catch her, the friend, calm as ever, simply said, 'I told you she would be fine!' I could have hit him. Matters didn't improve over the next weeks and months. In many ways they became worse as we realised that Sadie's preference for wandering rather than being with people, was a much deeper default setting than we could ever have imagined.

At this point I will give you some background about the new home to which Sadie had come. There were four of us in our family, myself, Jane, my husband Simon, and our two children, George, aged 23 and Alice aged 21. We lived on a small farm of 70 acres six miles outside Bridgnorth in Shropshire. The farmhouse was a bungalow which was divided into two. We lived in one half of the house and in the other lived my mother, a lifelong dog lover who had just lost her last dog. The farm was totally grassland and we had a flock of 100 ewes, two horses and several cats.

Jess had loved the cats and, when Sadie arrived, they thought she would follow in her predecessor's footprints; she didn't. It was sad, but Sadie didn't like them at all. Later she would tolerate them but for now she couldn't abide them. On the other hand, she obviously liked horses and sheep. There is always the fear when you get a dog with an unknown background, especially one which has a tendency to run free, that they are, or will become, sheep worriers. Even after a few days we could see this wasn't going to happen. She would lie down with either the sheep or the horses and both of them seemed perfectly happy to have her in their midst. It was very strange.

We knew the importance of hefting an animal so that it would identify the place it was in as home, from a couple of cats we acquired. We had a flock of free range hens at the time and with hens come rats. We struggled to keep them under control until a farmer friend suggested we had some cats. Funnily enough he happened to have two adult cats which he would let us have and he could bring them round the next day. You must, the farmer said, shut them up for two weeks or they will run off, but after this period they will be fine. The cats were brought in a sack and put in a shed and fed and watered there for two weeks, but when the time came for releasing them, far from stopping and sniffing their surroundings, they ran as fast as they could, across the field and into a large wood. I despaired of ever seeing them again, but I did notice that over the weeks that followed a number of rabbit skins had been left perfectly clean in the woods. The children were the first to discover why there were so many pelts - the cats had had kittens. It was hard to know how many there were as you couldn't get near them. As I started to feed the cats in the field, I saw the tabby cat with three kittens, and after a few days the ginger cat crept cautiously out of the woods with two more kittens. In a short space of time we had gone from no cats at all to two cats and five kittens. What a nightmare. I knew my husband would be furious as this was not part of the plan and, although I was not to blame, somehow it would be my fault and in consequence I must take responsibility for it. This was exactly what happened. Simon refused to acknowledge the rapid expansion of our cat population which could soon become considerably more if action wasn't taken to prevent the female cats getting pregnant again. My mother took charge and together we caught the cats and to the vet just in time as all the female cats were pregnant.

Sadie and the cats had much in common, both preferring freedom and the outdoor life but this lifestyle carried the risk of being run over. Somehow she had to be persuaded to stay closer to the humans whose company she despised. I turned for help to a friend, Carol, who was a dog trainer and the next day she gave us our first training session at the farm.

3

TRAINING

I would hide behind a tree in the hope of catching Sadie as she ran past

It appeared that I was doing a lot wrong, including having Sadie on a long lead which gave her the impression that she was in charge. She was quite correct about that, of course! Firstly, I must have her on a short lead and get her used to walking at my side. By rewarding this behaviour Sadie would be encouraged to walk to heel. The theory was great but we never did manage to put it into practice. For now both Sadie and I had our homework and Carol would return in a few days to see how things were going.

The next session highlighted the problem we had; our pupil had gone missing, having escaped through an open window. We spent two hours looking for her but she was nowhere to be found. Sadie was an escapologist par excellence. Her preference was to exit via windows rather than doors. No sooner had a window opened than Sadie spotted it and off she would go. In the early days we would run after her, partly in the hope of catching her (which we never did), and partly because of the fear of where she might run to - across the road and cause an accident or get in amongst the sheep and cause havoc. In fact, like the cats, she ran towards the wood and away from the road. She could then follow the woods for miles without being in any danger.

Meanwhile dog training was continuing. I had joined lessons in a nearby village hall with high hopes; well, with hopes anyway. There were about eight dogs, mainly youngsters, and Sadie was excited. Clearly this was a party and she couldn't wait for it to get started. When the party did start, the games were much more tame than her woodland walks. We formed a circle, each dog sitting on the left of their owner and then walking by his or her side to heel. I knew that I must practise between lessons and when working off the lead I took Sadie to the local tennis courts which provided an enclosed area.

While not perfect, she sat and stayed and came to me when called. Recognising that she couldn't get away she was compliant but in the open it was the same old story. Of course I was also getting stick from my husband about what a waste of time the training was and why I even bothered going to the lessons. I had the same misgivings but the truth was I didn't have an option.

Over the weeks that followed, most of the dogs learned basic obedience - sit, stay, come back, walk off the lead, lie down; all the things a dog and his/her owner need to know. Sadie also appeared to be doing well. In reality, as I pointed out to the trainers, she did the right thing by copying the dog in front. The result was that when, after two months, our progress was assessed, we failed. I sat disconsolately while rosettes were handed out to those who had passed. My encouragement, such as it was, was to repeat the course. 'I'm sure she will do better next time,' the trainer said enthusiastically, 'she has already improved so much.' I couldn't quite see this improvement but we repeated the course and once again failed the test. Again I was urged not to give up but half way through the third round of the same course the trainers themselves gave up on both of us and suggested that we didn't return.

It is the sheer loneliness of dealing with a difficult dog which is one of the hardest things. Not all difficult dogs come from rescue centres, of course, but when they do it would be nice to feel there was some sort of support. In the case of the centre I had Sadie from I had the distinct impression that, after an initial conversation, they just didn't pick up the phone to my subsequent calls. This might be unfair, but for whatever reason, there would be no help from that direction. Sadie, the champion of freedom, seemed to be unstoppable and the months of training had been a complete waste of time and money.

I tried to work out what was wrong with this dog and why she behaved as she did. Her behaviour was certainly odd in many ways. In July, when we went on holiday, we put Sadie in kennels for a fortnight. I went with my daughter to collect her and we were excited. We expected that the dog would feel the same way, but there was no interest in us whatsoever. We could have been complete strangers. As we walked her to the car, without warning she jumped straight onto the bonnet and then onto the roof. She stood proudly surveying the scene then jumped off as though this was normal. Farmer friends offered helpful advice; 'just have her put down, Jane.' The kindly dog trainer suggested that she would perhaps be better in a new home. I was mortified at the thought. Pig-headed, proud, selfish, call it what you will, I wasn't ready to give up yet.

There was also another dynamic in the situation. Since the disappointment of the first meeting, my husband had begun to love this little dog. Quietly, Simon had been forming a bond with her. Sadie had won his heart. Although he couldn't let her off the lead he took her with him when he was working around the farm, tying her up so that he could get on with his work. Whenever he went in the Landrover to visit his friends he would take Sadie with him. She leapt about the car excitedly and on visiting the nearby post office one day Sadie managed to lock the car with her and the keys inside. This amused him greatly; me less so, as I had to stop my work and take the spare keys.

There was also a glimmer of hope that Sadie could become a good working dog if, and this was a very big if, we could stop her running off. It was June and Simon had picked me up from the market. As we arrived home we could see that someone had left a gate open and all the sheep were in the hay field. Sadie was our best hope of getting the sheep out. I took her into the field, still on a long lead and something remarkable happened. Well, two things to be precise. Firstly, it was clear that Sadie understood that she had to move these sheep, and for their part the flock just as clearly got the message. The sheep who were never worried by Jess, recognising her to be a pushover, didn't feel the same way about Sadie. In theory, as they were happy for her to lie down with them they shouldn't have bothered about her at all but in practice they did. It was the weirdest thing. As soon as Sadie was in the field, the sheep immediately flocked together and moved as fast as they could back to their field. I was amazed. Sadie, like a really good sheepdog had appeared to do little. We had seen a very different side to her.

But while Sadie was loving and friendly in the house and when she couldn't get away, once on the loose she was a different dog. To match her split personality, she seemed to have two owners as well. When she was with Simon she was clearly his dog, but when she ran off, she mysteriously belonged to me. 'Your dog's gone again,' was a familiar greeting when I came back after a hard day's work on the market stall. No matter how inconvenient it was I had to stop what I was doing and go searching for Sadie. Farms are excellent sponges, of time as well as money, but why I should have more time than my husband to go looking for the dog was something of a mystery. This repetitive searching was becoming another job, the last thing I needed, and Sadie was becoming a very tedious job indeed.

Knowing where Sadie was, was one thing, catching her was another matter. She would spend all her time in the woods and my only chance of catching her was to hide behind a tree where the track went along a narrow ledge. Here there was a steep hill on one side and a cliff falling away to a stream on the other and if I was lucky I could grab her as she went past. I can't remember how I found this trick, but thank goodness I did. If I missed her it could be two hours before she went along this route again; enough time to go home and have a cup of tea, before returning to have another attempt. Once caught, Sadie always looked surprised to see me and the way she literally stopped dead in her tracks made me smile. I can only assume she was in a world of her own, enjoying the pleasures of the natural world we humans can't even dream of. I couldn't blame Sadie for wanting to spend all her time in this paradise, but the arrangement was that she should be part of our world and at the moment I was an inconvenient part of hers. We needed to be a partnership, a team, and we were as far away from that as we had been when we first met.

It was time to call in another expert. I saw an article in the local newspaper written by a dog psychologist and as the only such person I knew, I rang him up. Yes, he could certainly help. His fee was £95. That was a fortune for me as I was struggling to make ends meet and I had already spent that amount on the training classes. I restrained myself from saying, '£95, you have got to be joking,' because if he could stop Sadie running off it would be a good investment. It was agreed he would come round the following week. 'Take the dog out on the field on a long lead,' he said, and then took Sadie from me, made her stay, and then walked away to the opposite end of the lead. He called her to him and rewarded her with a treat. Several times he did this and she performed beautifully coming to him instantly each time, but one thing he didn't do, was to let her go completely, always there was the long lead attached. 'There is nothing wrong with this dog,' he declared, and the consultation was over. Time taken - 45 minutes. Was that what I got for my £95? Yes, that was it. There was no more. And was the problem solved? Of course it wasn't. I emailed him repeatedly without a reply and then about two months later he did answer having just returned from a holiday in Australia. With the fees he charged he could afford to travel Business Class! I gave him my opinion of his skills in dog psychology and that was the last I heard from him.

4

SIGNS OF IMPROVEMENT

The farm was a dog's paradise as far as the eye could see

We were now well into Autumn and to understand what happened next, you need to know that the farm income was derived from two sources. There was the income from the sheep, which was my husband's and the income from a business making and selling preserves, which was mine. I made the preserves every week at the farm and sold them each Saturday at the local market. It might sound like a nice cottage-type business but this was hard manual labour with very small returns. Before the preserves business we had a flock of three hundred free range hens when totally out of the blue, in December 1988, Edwina Currie made her pronouncement that most of the eggs produced in this country were infected with salmonella. The effect was almost instant. One week we had a nice free range egg business, the next we had nothing. That's not quite true, we had less than nothing, because the birds had to be fed but there was no market for the eggs. It was a hard decision but I had to have an income immediately, not in a year's time when the politicians had come up with new regulations. So the hens were replaced by the preserves business, and a new poly-tunnel was erected where we could grow vegetables. Emotionally it was devastating and I can't say it was a perfect solution to our shortage of money. The market for home-grown vegetables was as fickle as the egg market and all too often they became sheep fodder.

The preserves business peaked at Christmas time and having to stop work and go and catch a dog was the last straw. The busiest market was the Saturday before Christmas and I had returned absolutely worn out. About eight o'clock my mother came in and said she had let Sadie out. Thinking she was being helpful, mother was blissfully unaware of the consequences of this as she was suffering from dementia. Sadie would be long gone now so there was no point in going to look for her. Instead, I did two things; firstly I fired off the email to the psychologist, and secondly, I took a different tack and tried to work out why the dog ran off.

The dog trainers thus far had looked at the relationship between me and the dog and my inadequacies as a trainer. I might have agreed with them but the relationship would only work if I understood why the dog was behaving as it did. Dogs are like people; they are not all the same and each breed has different characteristics. I thought I understood collies a little, but Sadie was different. Firstly, there was her breeding, which, as I said at the beginning, was unknown, and secondly, there was the way she had been treated for the first seven months of her life, again unknown. All we had to go on was the dog's behaviour we saw now; but at least that was consistent. There was the daily running off and refusal to come back, a preference for windows rather than doors to make her exit (and even her entrance) and a preference for other animals for company rather than people. As I began to look more closely at the problem I was also aware that she didn't discriminate between various tones of the voice. The encouragement of, 'good dog,' had the same response as a more strident and desperate, 'here, Sadie.' To both, she turned her back and off she went. The distance Sadie created between herself and the rest of the family was both physical and psychological, but why?

Having ruled out deafness, I wondered if she was autistic. I had no idea if there were autistic dogs, but it seemed a possible explanation. On the other hand, when confined to the house or on a lead, this was a happy, responsive dog. In fact she was an absolute nuisance as she wanted constant attention. She seemed to love anyone who would love her, so autism was out! Diagnosis helps but sometimes you can't have anything conclusive, just vague hypotheses to work with. We had worked for nine months with the hypothesis that Sadie was just a free spirit but perhaps there was something else going on. What if the previous owners had responded to her running off by shutting her in and shouting at her. One couldn't blame them if current behaviour was anything to go by. All the training thus far would then have overlain a deep-seated fear that the past would repeat itself. So her solution might have been to comply with instructions when she couldn't get away but run like hell when she could.

It was soon after Christmas when I had heard a man on local radio who advised listeners on how to deal with pet problems. I was struck by his common sense but rather alarmed by his somewhat abrupt responses when he thought the owners were responsible for the dogs' behaviour. As my last hope it was with some trepidation that I rang the trainer up (off air, I hasten to add) and thankfully he couldn't have been more kind. The solution, he explained, was to make coming back home and coming back to her owners more appealing than running off. It was so obvious! He worked with the dogs in the open (hence in the environment where the problem occurred) and yes, he had no doubt that he could stop the running off and he would be very willing to help. There was one issue - that he lived a long way away. He told me how he worked and advised me what to do. I said that I would give it a try but if it hadn't worked in the next few weeks we would be coming to see him. There was no charge for the consultation but this man gave me two gifts even he couldn't imagine - encouragement that the problem could be sorted out and encouragement that I could do it.

The thing about collies and sheepdogs of whatever ilk is that the dog has an instinct to work but must also be responsive to what the shepherd wants it to do. Dog and man must work together to get the job done. Sadie at the moment had no desire whatsoever to be in a partnership but we didn't know then how quickly that would change.

It wasn't long before I had a chance to test out my theory about Sadie being frightened of people's voices. When she ran off the next time I caught her from behind the tree as usual, and put the lead on but instead of words of encouragement, I walked her home in silence. The change was remarkable. Once in the house she was happy enough as usual but when the front door was opened, instead of disappearing into the blue yonder, she went in and out of the door as though it was a new trick she had just learnt. It was very weird and not at all what one would have expected. I seemed to have hit on Sadie's chief fear - the human voice.

This was the turning point with Sadie. From here on she was a dog that could be much more a part of our lives. She never lost her love of freedom and sometimes that would be a nuisance, but I suppose as time went on we trusted that she would return. Gradually she became very definitely Simon's dog and he would take her with him wherever he went.

5

ALL CHANGE

Against all the odds Sadie became an excellent, if somewhat unorthodox, sheepdog

No sooner had we half recovered from Christmas than we were into lambing and we had yet to see how Sadie would behave. It's certainly not a time to have a dog running loose whether one knows they are going to return or not. So against her wishes, Sadie had to spend more time indoors than she would have liked, sometimes with the company of cold little lambs put in front of the fire against the winter chills. She would lick them until you could see they were thinking, 'that's enough now, just let me sleep.'

The following year everything changed. It was April and mother's cleaner came to me and said that mother had been very confused all morning.' Oh, no, I thought, not another thing to be dealt with on top of a workload which was already overburdened by lambing. I kept a close eye on mother throughout the day, and by late evening it was clear that something was very wrong. I phoned the doctor and he asked me to wait at the end of the drive and he would be with me in 15 minutes. It was three quarters of an hour before he arrived, by which time I was frozen. It would have been nice had he been friendly and kind but he was curt and cold. Mother had probably had a stroke he said but there was nothing that could be done. I must say I was surprised because I thought the advice was to treat stroke patients in hospital as soon as possible. This was indeed the recommendation of mother's own doctor when I phoned the next morning. I followed the ambulance to the hospital and when I got there the first of the five doctors who were called in to decide if she had had a stroke was examining her. By the time the last doctor did the same, mother asked me what was going on. 'They are trying to decide whether you have had a stroke, I said.' 'Why does it take five of them to decide that?' she said. I had no answer. Mother had been a doctor at a time when she couldn't have called on one other doctor, let alone four, to confirm her decision. She had indeed had a stroke and was kept in hospital.

Anyone who has looked after someone with dementia will know the strain this imposes on a family, so with mother in hospital we were suddenly able to relax and enjoy a certain normality again. The freedom was wonderful but we didn't realise how short-lived this was to be. Just two weeks later, on Saturday morning, I went off to market as usual. Unexpectedly, about 11 o'clock, I had a phone call from my daughter to say that she had come into the kitchen and found Simon on the floor unconscious. What should she do? Phone for an ambulance I said and I will, of course, come straight home. In an instant like this everything fixes in your head. I was just serving a customer and offered the change. 'Keep it, you are going to need it,' she said. How right she was. I left the market stall in the hands of my assistant and as I turned to get my car an ambulance went by, lights and siren on. I knew where it was going.

When I got to the farm Simon was on a stretcher and conscious. I have no idea what I said at this point, it all happened so suddenly. The paramedics nodded at each other and indicated they knew what had happened. I did not. They sped off in the ambulance and as my daughter and I followed, she told the full story of what was to be a profound turning point in our lives.

The two of us sat in A&E and were called in to see my husband and be told what they proposed would be the next step. He had had an aortic aneurism and they suggested he should be transferred to Stoke Hospital. Simon shook his head vigorously. Fully conscious, he did not want to go. I reassured him that it would be the best thing and said something fatuous but can't remember what. I do, however, remember Simon's words; 'I've fed the lambs, look after them.' They were the last words he spoke.

Over the weekend Simon's condition deteriorated and despite the best efforts of the surgeons he died two days later. My son had come up from London and in the early morning of the May Bank Holiday Monday we arrived back home. A farmer friend had been to look after the sheep and feed Sadie and there she was to greet us.

Lambing was over but there was much work to be done so it was time to just carry on and, of course, arrange the funeral. The vicar came immediately on that Monday to see us and was a tower of strength. We cried, we laughed, and we drank lots of cups of tea. We could have done without all the flowers people brought us over the next week. Not only did we rapidly run out of vases, the flowers added to the abnormality of the situation. Between that Monday and the day of the funeral was a waiting period. It is a weird time; you can't move on but are stuck in a dutiful limbo and you make lots of cups of tea for people who sit around and make you feel even more miserable. No matter how we felt, there was a farm to run and we would feel a lot better if we did some work.

The funeral, as so often, was an uplifting blur. The man who gave the eulogy made everyone laugh but what made me laugh even more was that one farmer was overheard saying to another, 'It's a good job he finished the lambing before he died!' Ever practical are farmers.

When it was all over there we were on our own and, with my son returning to London, it was just my daughter who was at college locally, and myself, trying to juggle the demands of two businesses. Money was a pressing matter. It was simple - there wasn't any. As long as there was enough money to feed the sheep then Simon was happy. The problem was that whatever money the sheep made they ate. It was a vicious circle. The preserves business didn't make a huge amount of money nor did the sheep. Together they produced enough to live on but no more. Life was not going to be easy.

It was about two weeks after Simon died and I had gone out for the evening leaving my daughter and Sadie at home. When I returned there was no Sadie. A phone call to the police drew a blank, no dog had been handed in. The next morning, after a sleepless night, we started the hunt for Sadie again, this time with more success. A phone call to the local shop revealed that Sadie had been picked up by a couple who had left their phone number with the shopkeeper. I asked if the dog was all right, thinking she might be injured or had been killed but she was apparently absolutely fine. It transpired that Sadie had been standing in the middle of a busy main road about a mile away, and the couple had risked life and limb to save her. With vehicles rattling along that road at great speed, the man had literally picked her up and bundled her into the car. It wasn't hard to understood what Sadie was doing. She had gone looking for her master, taking the usual route that Simon took to visit his friends. Whether it was the noise of the traffic or the realisation that she was far from home which caused her to stand in the middle of the road, we will never know. Not for the first time, Sadie's sweet nature was her salvation. She got on well with the couple's other dogs and cheekily slept all night on her rescuers' bed. The next morning the man took Sadie to work with him and she curled up and went to sleep. Clearly Sadie was content with her new friends and I had an uncomfortable decision to make. The couple wanted to keep Sadie and for her part it seemed that the dog would be quite happy to stay. The husband in particular had fallen in love with her and the decision I had to make was whether it was in the dog's best interest to let them keep her or to have her back. I thought long and hard and I turned for advice to the dog trainer who had helped me earlier. He made sense of the situation from Sadie's point of view. Because Simon had died in hospital the dog didn't know he had died and so went looking for him. I must say I found the idea of a dog going to look for her master and bring him home absolutely heartbreaking. However the trainer assured me that if I put some of her master's clothing in her basket she would settle. I made my decision. A good sheep dog was going to be essential and the thought of getting and training a new dog on top of everything else was too much. The couple brought Sadie back later that day. They were upset to part with her but there it was. I needed this little dog, it was as simple as that.

Sadie had become a very valuable asset as a sheepdog. What she lacked in finesse she made up for in enthusiasm. Whatever the weather and whatever the job, she was happy to work. The sheep surrendered before this tiny dog that moved so fast they never quite knew where she was. And after her job was done, she would then wait quietly while the humans did theirs. This was the only time when her wanderlust was put on hold and if she was ever impatient and thought, 'I wish you would hurry up, I have other things to do,' she never showed it. She followed in her master's footsteps. The sheep were more important to Sadie than anything else.

6

BRIGHTENING FROM THE WEST

Friends rallied round to help which sometimes involved some serious dog training

On a day when it was hammering down with rain and there was not a break in the clouds, Simon would often say ironically, 'it's brightening from the West'. It's a reminder that dark nights don't always end in bright dawns.

My mother, far from recovering from the stroke, had deteriorated both mentally and physically and the hospital announced one day that she wouldn't be able to return home. They offered to send her immediately to a care home where there happened to be a bed. I recognised that the staff saw me as more of a soft touch than my sister but even I could smell a rat in their enthusiasm for the idea and how easily it could be implemented. 'Transport can be arranged this afternoon,' they said. I replied that I was not prepared to give an answer until I had spoken to my sister. 'Definitely not,' she said, 'not until we have been to this care home and approved it ourselves.'

From the outside it was clear that the home had once been a workhouse and inside that the poor and infirm of Victorian times had been replaced by a group with severe mental health issues who shuffled from room to room accompanied by two care assistants. The atmosphere of aggression was tangible, hence presumably the need to keep the group on the move. I recognised one of the men, for they were all men, and turned to talk to him. Of course he wouldn't recognise me but I wanted to offer a smile and share a little of how I knew him. It was all I could do. Then we were taken to see the bedrooms, cells unchanged from workhouse days.

There was no mistaking that these were cells. They were small and narrow with heavy doors into which a small window had been cut for ease of inspection and there were bars on the inside of the windows. I imagined how terrifying it would be to sleep in one of these rooms, even for, perhaps especially for, someone with dementia. These were not rooms with en-suite facilities and it struck me that the substantial doors might have also protected the patients from night time visitors? It didn't bear thinking about.

While I was shocked, my sister was not. A history of illness over many years had given her a view of a range of hospital facilities, good and bad. Her conclusion, with which I agreed, was that mother wouldn't last a week here. Eventually, when mother was placed in a care home without bars on the bedroom doors, there was still more than a sense of the prison about it. 'Home' was now the first floor of a house from which it was impossible to escape even into the lovely gardens which surrounded it. It was hard to accept that mother would never again be allowed to walk outside the confines of this building whenever she wanted, that she would never again enjoy the sun on her face. Freedom was restricted to a bedroom and one large room in which residents ate and were constantly 'entertained' by two televisions blaring out from opposite ends of the room. Watched only by staff who would snatch glimpses of programmes as they went about their work, the televisions made for difficult conversation. And there my mother sat all day, dressed sometimes in her own clothes, sometimes in someone else's, talking quietly to herself and asking what everyone was doing in her house.

One day I decided I would take some of the normality of the outside world into the Home. Sadie was to accompany me because I thought a dog would perk mother up. I also thought that Sadie would enjoy the attention since she could never get enough love. Perhaps it was the impossibility of escape, the very definite smell in the air, or the moaning and shouting, which unnerved her. Whatever the reason, Sadie was ill at ease and just couldn't settle. As soon as she went in the room she wanted to be out again. The visit was not a success.

Back at the farm I had a clear goal, to make enough money so that I could keep the farm. The deal was this. The farm was in a trust and when my mother died it would have to be sold and the proceeds split between the three children. Having paid no rent for many years I had no right to remain unless I could pay the selling price. To do that, serious money had to be made. As long as mother was alive my position was secure, the unthinkable would happen when she died.

At least I thought that my position was secure until I received a letter from the Council shortly after mother went into a care home threatening that the farm would have to be sold immediately to pay the fees. It seemed that I had no rights in this situation and the prospect of imminent homelessness was terrifying. I had already experienced this authoritarianism when a Weights and Measures Inspector paid me an impromptu visit just two days after Simon had died. In spite of my explanation of the circumstances, the visit continued without comment, and with every piece of kitchen equipment being measured. By law I had no right to refuse access but this was ridiculous! The Council's threat to sell the farm hung over me for weeks before the matter was resolved. In fact there were ample funds for the fees to be paid without selling the farm but it was a salutary reminder, not that I needed one, of how tenuous my position was.

Somehow I had to concentrate on the present; the farm had to be run and the preserves to be made. For now, even paying the bills was hard enough, but in the long term I clung to the hope of making enough money to be able to keep the farm. The problem was that I didn't know how long I had to make the money necessary, that depended on how long mother lived. Half the house was empty so I could, in theory, capitalise on that, but there could be no security of tenure.

There was no time to lose and a successful businessman offered to give my daughter and myself some consultancy advice as to how we might increase our income. It was exciting to think that there might be a fresh approach but whatever he suggested I had either tried or put forward reasons why I thought it wouldn't work. Over several weeks he hid his frustration until one day he turned his attention from product to personality. In his view, I was not receptive to new ideas and a hindrance to progress. 'I think', he said, 'that you should hand the business over to your daughter.' I hadn't seen that coming and it was a shock which reduced me to tears. I had never thought of myself as someone who was devoid of ideas nor as one who shied away from carrying them out. To be told by someone that they saw you as exactly the opposite kind of person from who you see yourself to be was devastating. After a swift departure from the room, I returned with my decision. I was not about to hand over the reins of the business. The consultations were at an end.

Small farms like ours were an anachronism fifty years ago. What used to be family farms were suddenly called hobby farms in recognition of the fact that they could no longer support a family. Now 200 acres is thought small yet at one time this would have produced a good income for a family. Unless you have a niche product, diversification is the only option. Were the opportunities ever there? Five years earlier, perhaps, but five years earlier, in 2001, Foot and Mouth had locked us down; hardly the best time for forging a bright future. To make matters worse, I had hitched our wagon to the organic sector whose growth in our part of the country was non-existent. With no organic market we ended up paying a big price for organic registration and could only sell our produce non-organically. Cost and no benefit - brilliant.

The best chance of getting cash seemed to be to sell some ewes and lambs. I knew that a dealer would give me immediate payment but I have always been wary of dealers, and of auctions for that matter. It is a deep-seated mistrust which comes from my father's experience. Father ran an antique shop in a local town with his father. A lot of the stock was, of course, bought at auctions and father was asked to join a ring of dealers.

They worked like this. Before the auction, a number of buyers (the ring) would agree who was going to buy which lot and at what price. After the auction had ended, the dealers would (unofficially and illegally) have a second auction when the lot was resold. Father vehemently refused to join the ring and told the dealers exactly what he thought of their practices. I suspect that the dealers then conspired against my father, trotting up the price for the lots he wanted until it was unviable to buy the item. The shop was soon struggling financially and eventually it closed.

In the 1980s and 1990s, dealer's rings, although illegal, were still thriving. One of my husband's best friends was a dealer and it was often hard to listen to the stories of how money was made. In one case a farmer was leaving the market having sold his stock at below the price he expected. By chance he came across the reason; a group of dealers were holding their own auction for the lots their members had bought. The farmer's lot was one of those and he was so angry he was ready for a fight. It was with difficulty that one of the dealers in the ring took the farmer to one side and reasoned with him, saying that he was making a fool of himself. How dare they, for they were the ones in the wrong and he the injured party. As the story was retold to me by the dealer himself I couldn't help wishing the farmer had punched one of them on the nose.

So this explains why I had to have been pretty desperate when, in June, I asked a dealer to look at the lambs with a view to giving me a price. It was frightening letting a stranger into this world I had so recently taken charge of and I braced myself for the meeting. I knew it wasn't going to be easy. Being a local man he would know how much I needed the money and I had to be careful not to show how vulnerable my position really was. After a look at the sheep the dealer delivered his judgment. 'They're very plain them sheep,' he said. Seeing my disappointment he added, 'I expect it's the weather - it's been a difficult year, very dry and cold. My lambs haven't put on as much as they should.' 'So what do you think then, how much are they worth,' I asked. 'As they stand, about £20 a life.' I restrained my indignation, and calmly clarified the price. 'A life, you mean the same for a ewe as a lamb?' 'Yes, £40 for a ewe and a lamb,' he answered. This was a lot worse than I had imagined. While I needed the money, I wasn't going to give the livestock away. I refused the offer and kept the sheep.

Farmer friends already stretched in running their own farms rallied round to help and somehow got me through the major jobs such as shearing, selling lambs and haymaking. It was an amazing network of support without which I don't know what I would have done.

In June, after Simon died, my daughter asked me if she might have a dog. Simon would only have collies but Alice wanted a spaniel. I confess that a new dog was not what I needed at the moment but agreed. Evie, a Springer Spaniel arrived; two handfuls of fur, lonely, confused and wondering what had happened to her. How would Sadie react? Evie was gently put in front of the fire and to our amazement Sadie fetched her toys and put them in front of her new friend. It was extraordinary and the two dogs did indeed become the best of friends. Sadie would still run off and now she had a friend to accompany her on her travels. That had to be stopped or both would be killed on the road. In due course, I took Evie to dog training classes and she was as easy to train as Sadie had been difficult.

In the autumn my daughter who had been working with me in the kitchen told me she would be going on holiday to Australia for six weeks just prior to Christmas. The timing couldn't have been worse; the busiest time of the year. Fortunately my son came back from London for this period so we got by. When my daughter returned she was cross to see that her dog had been allowed certain liberties such as sleeping on the furniture. It was the least of my worries.

My main worry at this time was lack of cash. I looked around for something to sell and the most promising were two paintings which my father had been given many years before. My son and I took them to be valued at the local auction house which held art sales. The auctioneer was enthusiastic and had no doubt that one painting should sell for between £2,500 and £3,000 and the other for between £700 and £800. We agreed that they would be entered in the next art sale in November and looked forward to the day. This was a full day's sale and we sat at the back and watched the proceedings. At the start of the day we were encouraged, there were no other similar paintings and ours looked like the quality they were. The sale room was full of buyers but it was soon apparent that there were mixed fortunes for the items up for sale. It was also abundantly evident that most of the buyers were there to bid for art works by well-known twentieth century artists. As the day wore on the buyers drifted away and our paintings had yet to be sold. The small painting managed to reach its reserve of £700 but the large painting was the last lot to be sold by which time there were only about three people left in the room and there was no bid. We collected the painting and took it home. The auctioneer was genuinely sorry it didn't sell and was certain it would sell on another day. Once again another day wouldn't do, I needed cash now and not in three months time. I reflected that, even if the large painting had sold at the top of its estimate, the money wouldn't have helped my situation much. I kept the painting, which I still have today, and have never regretted that decision.

Work was relentless, and coming up to Christmas I could have worked for 24 hours a day and still not have finished. As if there wasn't enough work to do, there was also wood to collect for the log burner, the only form of heat in my part of the house. Ah, the joy of a log burner when the wood is dry and well-seasoned and the misery on dank days when it doesn't want to go at all. It had been one of those days, when the damp cold air of autumn hung around as a fog and daylight couldn't break through the gloom. My working day had started at 6 am and finished at 9 pm, not unusual for farmers, but by the end of it I was exhausted and hungry.

Unfortunately, there was little in the fridge to eat, the house was freezing and it was a 5.30 start in the morning. Going to bed immediately seemed the best option. An unexpected knock at the door changed that idea, for there stood a man who came lamping for rabbits, and he was bearing gifts! 'My wife has been baking some pies and she thought you might like these,' he said, as he handed over three hot pigeon and steak pies which his wife had just made. Then he was on his way again, out into the cold Autumn night, to keep down our plentiful stock of rabbits. I settled down to eat one of the pies and I have to say it was one of the best meals I have ever had. 'Little unremembered acts of kindness,' as Wordsworth so beautifully put it.

Christmas was a celebration of survival but my plans for making some serious money were hampered by the tenuous situation I was in. With no security of tenure, any plans, short, medium or long-term, were impossible. At the same time I was trapped here in this seemingly inescapable limbo. On Alice's return from holiday, she needed to find a business or career of her own. We had looked at a variety of business options but nothing seemed workable. By the New Year Alice very sensibly decided that she would have to find employment elsewhere.

7

2006 A LITTLE OPTIMISM

I looked across at a landscape which meant so much to me but would my efforts to keep it be in vain?

My daughter's job led to new friends and a decision to move to the south of England. I really was on my own now, just myself and the two dogs. It is at times like this that one realises (if you ever doubted it) the importance of a good dog. Evie was such an obedient, quiet and gentle dog and Sadie a good complement. They were my rocks.

Sadie was now a very proficient sheep dog who instinctively understood what she needed to do. I would like to say she was working in response to commands but I can't be sure that was the case. I would have preferred the sheep to be moved rather more slowly than as if it were a timed sheepdog trial but I wasn't complaining. Sadie was doing well.

The dogs enjoyed themselves on the farm, running as free as a dog should. It was dog heaven. As spring approached I was working out in the fields one day when Evie had quite a fright. She suddenly leapt into some bracken and proudly came out with a grass snake, still curled up, which had been basking to get warm. I don't know who was more surprised. It was a big snake, and as I called Evie away, off it went, apparently none the worse for the experience. A slow learner, Evie was about to repeat this the next time we were out. I called her away, of course, for this might have been an adder and she might not have been so lucky.

Evie's real pleasure came from chasing rabbits and the odd pheasant that had survived the winter shoots. Sadie's quarry was of a different order; she loved to chase foxes. The chances of her catching one (and what would she do if she did) were minimal, but the job required working the night shift just as I was ready for bed. At the last 'let-out' of the day, Sadie would invariably hear or smell a fox and she was off. Evie chose not to follow but Sadie's excited cries could be heard as she ran through the woods and off into the distance. Waiting for Sadie to return (at about one or two o'clock in the morning) was pointless so I would go to bed and leave her to come in when the hunt was over. I knew she would come to no harm in the woods and Evie and I needed our sleep.

In April 2006, I waited for a cheque for £2,000 from DEFRA through a new scheme called the Single Payments Scheme. I don't need to emphasise how much I needed the money. Designed to make the payment of subsidies more efficient it had missed its target spectacularly. Like most farmers across the country, I waited and waited, and made repeated phone calls to see when the money might arrive. Eventually it was apparent that DEFRA themselves had no idea when the money might be paid. This was a shambles for which the Department incurred a large fine but was no consolation to those whose payments were seriously delayed. I mentioned the situation in passing to an acquaintance at church. She rang and offered me the money as a loan. I said I couldn't possibly accept it, even though it would be paid back as soon as the subsidy money arrived. 'OK, you make your decision, but I will put the cheque in your letter-box and if you don't want to use it, tear it up.' I didn't tear the cheque up and was so grateful for the help. The loan kept me going until the DEFRA payment eventually arrived in the autumn. Without it I don't know what I would have done,

The market business, popular as it might be among customers, stubbornly refused to make anything approaching a living wage. I turned over a lot of money but it was a case of diminishing returns. The harder I worked and the more I sold, the less, proportionately, I made. I had looked for a way of making bigger profits and just before Simon died I received a large order which would do exactly that. The highs and lows of life. With Simon's death it was impossible to fulfil the order so it had to be declined. Normally I did every flower show, food fair, and market within a reasonable distance, but I couldn't do that with the extra responsibilities of the farm. Even a Saturday market would be a struggle.

I opened Mother's half of the house as a Bed and Breakfast and was so grateful to those who came but it wasn't easy. Most people's stay included a Saturday which meant that I had to be in two places at once - cooking breakfast and at the market. And the rewards, while getting me through another week, were a drop in the ocean compared with what I needed if I was going to keep the farm. I took every opportunity to work including as a speaker at local groups. One talk was to a women's group in the April after Simon had died. The venue was twenty miles away. It had seemed like such a good idea when I accepted the invitation but the weather worsened during the day and turned into a blizzard by late afternoon. To make matters worse, the ewe lambs from the previous year had just started lambing and they were all on the field. Any lambs born out in this weather wouldn't survive. One had already lambed on the field and I just had time to put ewe and lamb in the barn before I set off for the talk. Again I needed to be in two places at the same time and I was so tired. I expected to find the audience small or non-existent but to my amazement the room was full. As I was setting up, I overheard one of the organisers say to another, 'have you put the money up for the speaker.' 'Yes,' was the answer, 'I have put £20 in an envelope.' I can't deny that the thought of the money kept my spirits up more than somewhat, so imagine how I felt when, on opening the envelope at home, there was £10 in it!

This wasn't the way forward. I was wearing myself out without making any financial progress. Unexpectedly, early in the summer of 2006, I was rung up by Ed, a farmer friend with whom I played tennis. Completely unknown to me, several farmers had been talking about how they might help, and Ed was deputed to find out what was required.

I had many worries on the farm, one of which was the unglamorous topic of the septic tank. For the twenty years I had lived at the farm there had been an ongoing problem with the septic tank. Simon typically did a quick fix without solving the underlying problem. I had forgotten all about this when the first bed and breakfast guests were due to arrive. With perfect timing, all the drains around the house were blocked. I allowed myself a moment to think, 'I can't do this,' before setting to and sorting the problem out as we had done many times before. I couldn't risk this happening again so when Ed asked if he could help, this was where we started. We pored over plans of the drainage and tried to work out where the problem might be. Potentially this could have been a very expensive problem to resolve but it had to be done. A friend came with a digger to dig down to the pipes on the field and I went across the field to examine the problem with Sadie and Evie accompanying me. Evie, recognising someone she knew the other side of the deep trench, ran full pelt to greet Ed and dived straight into the hole. The miracle was that the earth didn't come in on top of her. The problem was a cracked pipe adjoining the septic tank, most probably cracked when the septic tank was built. This was possibly the least costly cause to resolve and resolved it was, once and for all. Would I have been able to do this on my own? I doubted it.

The next matter to be addressed was fencing and hedge cutting. Ed had a man working for him who he thought would be able to help me on a casual basis. I began to wonder at Ed's judgment when he brought Adam to meet me. My new farm worker was, without a doubt, the most languid man I have ever met. Although he was young and fit enough to do any of the jobs required, whether he had any inclination to do them was another matter. However, my choice of labourer was limited. People don't like getting their hands dirty these days and those who could do the job want huge amounts of money for so doing. Adam was prepared to work for a reasonable wage if, and it was a very big if, I could get him to work. From the start it was like another job to get Adam to work and his laziness irritated me beyond endurance. One of the jobs which needed doing was the felling of a number of trees, a two-man job. Adam mentioned that he had a friend who might be prepared to help. I feared that he might be an Adam clone but thankfully he was the exact opposite. Tim was a country man through and through, one of a dying breed whose skills have been handed down through the generations. Not only did Tim know how the jobs should be done, he was a grafter, and Adam worked under his instruction. Between the two of them, they did the hundred and one maintenance jobs that had been neglected over the years.

Gradually the farm was looking better and I was beginning to enjoy myself. The rent from part of the house had given me an income large enough to invest in improvements. New fences were put in, the old tractor having not worked since Simon died was replaced with one that did, and the sense of small achievements, albeit not reflected in cash, were cheering. I had a freedom to make choices and do what I thought was needed. It was good to feel that I was making a difference.

On the other hand there is a fine line between freedom and loneliness. Juggling all the work was wearing and the days were never long enough. There was very little time for any social life. While I had always been used to going out socially on my own, I realised shortly after Simon had died that it is very different being one of a couple from being single. Simon would invariably stay at home, preferring the company of his sheep and the dog rather than people. It was just a few weeks after Simon had died that I rather reluctantly went to a tennis club 'do.' As I walked in there was definitely an awkward atmosphere. I knew all the people there and was on good terms with them but there was no smile, no friendly wave - nothing. Those whose company I enjoyed on the tennis court simply turned and stared. I was beating a hasty retreat (a night with Sadie was definitely more appealing than this) but as I was edging towards the door to leave, a friendly face said, 'come and join us, Jane.' Had I changed so much in the space of a few weeks? No, but my circumstances had. Why being single and going out on my own was different from being married and doing the same I have no idea. I could only observe that it was so and make sure I didn't repeat the experience.

Work kept me going but I was soon to be reminded that there were others in the equation who had to be looked after. I was in the kitchen working happily away one day, when a friend arrived with Sadie. I was surprised that Sadie was with him because I thought she was safely in the house. I can only suppose she had slipped out as was her old habit. At first I thought Pete had just come to see me. Shortly after Simon died, Pete and his wife came and said, 'We've come to help. I don't know what we can do, but just put us to work.' That time had long gone, so I hadn't expected to see Pete on the doorstep. He explained that he had been driving in a different direction, on a different road when for no obvious reason, he knew he must go down the road in front of the house. This would take Pete out of his way, but fortunately he did as he was 'told,' and was amazed to see Sadie standing in the middle of the main road looking lost. She was so pleased to see him and happily got in his car. It was a salutary lesson that if someone else was looking after Sadie, I must take more care of her as well.

8

THE BEGINNING OF THE END

Some go to farm sales to capture a bargain others are there simply to enjoy themselves

In January 2007 I received the phone call I was dreading. My mother was in hospital and not expected to live. My mother died on the morning that Ed came over to discuss my next move. I remember my words. 'My mother has died; I have failed.' At that point I had lost my mother, my home and my livelihood. There was nothing more to be said.

The farm had been bought by my mother in the late 1960s and run by my father on a part-time basis at first.

When my father died in 1980 mother didn't want to stay on the farm on her own and asked my husband if we would move in. By this time, in addition to our full time jobs, we had a flock of hens and a small flock of sheep. This explains how, twenty-seven years later, I was living in a house which I neither owned nor rented.

The sale of the farm was nothing to do with me, that was for the solicitor to arrange but there were two assets I owned which had a choice to keep, or not, the dogs. Evie, I was pretty sure, would settle anywhere, but Sadie had transformed herself into a working dog. Should I put her up for rehoming so that she could stay on a farm? I spoke to Ed about whether the dogs would ever settle off the farm. His reply was instant. 'The dogs will be happy wherever you are, Jane.' That was enough, I resolved to keep the dogs.

Nonetheless, some different training was in order. The dogs had hardly been away from the farm. My daughter had once taken Sadie to a local beauty spot for a walk where there were a lot of people. Sadie simply refused to walk and made it quite plain that the sooner she got back in the car and went home, the better pleased she would be. It was a quirk of her character that Sadie hated being anywhere where there were crowds but wherever we were going to live it was likely the dogs would have to go for walks on leads and they would certainly meet more people than they had until now. Would Sadie ever adapt? The first walk was pretty nerve racking as I had no idea when, or if, Sadie would return when she was let off the lead. I decided to take the dogs up a hill on leads and then release them at the top so that I would be able to see what Sadie was doing. I also needed to be sure that if we came across sheep in open country she wouldn't decide to gather them and bring them to me. In fact, when we did meet them she just looked at me as if to say, 'well, what do you want me to do?' And when told to leave them, she immediately obeyed. Sadie had a remarkable instinct for understanding what she was supposed to do with sheep. In that regard only did we have a working partnership, in every other way, Sadie's free spirit ruled. Foxes and deer were fair game and no-one would stop her enjoyment of the chase.

The only thing to do now was to plan the sale of everything on the farm. I was certain of one thing, that I was not going to have a farm sale. In many ways this would have been the easiest solution, but chance plays too big a part in whether the sale is successful or not for my liking. My father had once decided to rent a couple of fields by auction. It was a spring evening and there were a number of similar lots up for rent on other farms in the area. On the evening of the sale it poured with rain and no-one came. I remember my father's excitement in anticipation of the sale and the work he put into preparation. What a contrast it was when he walked into the house afterwards, carrying his disappointment on his shoulders. Perhaps the signs were in his face but coward that I was I took care not to look too closely. I understood now how he had needed that money.

I had also been to enough sales of 'Live and Dead Stock' to know that I was not up to the ordeal. I remember a young woman lining up the tractors for sale, with tears streaming down her face. That was the last farm sale I ever went to and I knew I just couldn't do it. Incidentally, 'dead stock' is the archaic description given to inanimate objects. The auctioneers who conduct the dispersal sale organise all the objects to be sold into lots. Starting with items of lowest value, old timber or scrap, the sale progresses until every object, including livestock, is accounted for.

On the day of the auction, the field where the sale is to take place is transformed into a cross between a car boot sale and a fair. Firstly, the auctioneer and his assistants arrive, together with a catering van, and the potential buyers and hangers-on, for this is as much an entertainment for the audience as a place for making serious purchases. With no intention of buying anything, many are there simply to enjoy themselves, to meet their friends, and have a nose in nooks and crannies they wouldn't normally see. Others add to the banter as each lot is sold while buyers quietly get on with their business. Amongst this jumble of comedians, neighbours, friends, buyers and auctioneers, the seller has, of course, the most to gain or lose on this day. There is no going back. It is a day when life as it was may be exchanged for an uncertain future.

The sale of livestock is emotionally the hardest and sometimes even the buyers can't bear to watch. I remember being at a sale when the last lot was in the cowshed. The auctioneer encouraged those who were interested to follow him. 'Ladies and gentlemen would you like to follow me to the cowshed where I will sell the sheepdogs.' My husband and I were not the only ones who couldn't bear to witness that.

At home, the fields and woods which I had loved walking became an immense sadness as I knew I wouldn't be walking them for much longer. Now I had to plan the unravelling of a way of life. The fact remained that all the assets of the farm that were mine had to be disposed of one way or another. Ed had played his part in helping me plan a future on the farm but now I was on my own.

Over the next few months everything I had was sold, including the sheep, poly-tunnels, and the tractor which I had not long bought. Selling the sheep was the most bitter of blows and the farm was desolate without any livestock. The last harvest was definitely a time to take a firm grip on my emotions. Arrangements for selling the farm were dealt with by mother's solicitor as the property was held in trust, but it made sense that I was the one who dealt with the estate agent and prospective purchasers. In August, viewings were arranged over a weekend. There were a lot of people; the curious and the serious, strangers and those I knew, and those who had plans for the property beyond my imagination. I took the potential buyers across the fields and through the woods, the dogs accompanying us, of course. The eventual buyer came into the category of having designs on the property which were unimaginable. Of course they didn't share their intentions but effectively they wanted to use the land as a tip. When the new buyers eventually moved in, every valley, whether grassland or ancient woodland, was obliterated by tons of earth (one hopes) being dumped there. The heartbreak and guilt which this invoked was yet to come, my immediate problem was where on earth was I going to live?

Without any capital to buy a house, I soon found that with two dogs, renting was out of the question; one dog would have been fine, two, absolutely not. This was 2007, the height of the property boom, and landlords could pick and choose their tenants. Ed suggested that I should buy a house with an agricultural tie but these were few and far between and the problem of lack of capital remained. Between the new buyers moving into the farm and the solicitor providing me with the means to buy a house, I could be homeless. It was a chilling thought and there seemed to be no solution.

This didn't stop well-meaning people trying to find me a house. One friend was particularly diligent, bombarding me daily with new finds. Online estate agents can be a mixed blessing. Too polite to say, 'For God's sake stop,' viewings were arranged at innumerable houses. The more I saw the more dispirited I became. Being someone else's project wasn't helpful. I was in a state of mental paralysis. Even if I had the funds to buy, I couldn't see myself living anywhere else and with no ties to a place, I could live anywhere or nowhere. Would there ever be a place I would fit in?

I had to shake myself out of this state of mind or I really would be homeless. The predicament I was in concerned no-one else so no-one else was going to come up with a solution. The solicitor had his job to do, but that didn't go as far as helping me to find another home. Eventually I came up with a plan. I asked the solicitor if he could release me some money so that I could buy a house. I came up with a figure and the answer, surprisingly, was, 'yes, I think I can do that.' At last, and in the nick of time, I could begin to look for a house. The figure was large enough to buy me a nice house but not in the rural area I would have preferred to live in and certainly not in the parish where I was living. My choice was limited but I found a house in a quiet backwater. I remember saying to the owner, 'it's a nice house but I don't know if it's my house.' Eleven years later I am still here and my opinion is the same; it's a home but it's not my home. Perhaps there never will be anywhere which feels like home again.

A date was set for moving from the farm and packing up had to begin but apart from disposing of what I couldn't or wasn't going to take with me, I just couldn't bring myself to do anything. The same paralysis descended as had struck me when looking for a house. Then, with a week to go, and nothing packed for the move, I was laid low by the most dreadful cold. I happened to be speaking to some friends who had recently moved to Norfolk and their reply was instant. 'We'll come and help.' It was another generous gesture without which I really don't know what I would have done. When all was packed the friends went back home and for a week I was alone with the dogs. There was still much to do and I tried not to think about the future. On the day of the move, friends and family came and helped and as the removal van went down the drive it was my turn to leave. I put the dogs on their leads lest they take off over fields that were no longer mine, and I tried to look neither to the right or the left, but already the intentions of the new buyers were clear; two diggers were lined up in the field. Evidently no time was to be lost in changing the landscape. I can't describe what I felt at that moment in addition to the sadness of leaving. It was an unpleasant shock which I just hadn't seen coming.

9

SHE WAS HERE A MOMENT AGO

We wandered along green lanes until my feet ached and the surroundings began to feel a little more more like home

At the other end of my journey, a mere six miles away, was our new home, very different from the farm. There were houses all around, a lot of them, two of them overlooking my garden. There were street lights which were so hard to get used to after the darkness of the farm and the people were strangers. I knew no-one and no-one came to make my acquaintance.

Lest I seem ungrateful, I was not. We had a roof over our heads and a house that was mine. There was a lot to be said for that after having lived in someone else's house for a very long time. Moreover it was quiet; it was more than quiet, it was peaceful. And Ed had been right. The dogs seemed perfectly happy. They might have dreamt about the fields and woods we had lost, but it wasn't apparent.

One of the difficulties I had in settling in was the change in perspective from the farm. Instead of looking outwards towards the land, my gaze was turned inwards to the house. It was a big shift and would take some getting used to. On a positive note, if I could just see it, I had exchanged a few fields and some woods for a world waiting to be explored. I bought a map of the local area and books of suggested walks and off we went.

Before the village I was now living in was built, the area was a disused airfield which had been used in both the First and Second World Wars. In the late 1970s, housing development began and obliterated much of the airfield landscape which had been imposed on the farmland before it. Surprisingly, however, there was a lot of evidence of pre-war times and there were large areas of undeveloped land through which one could walk. There were tracks which predated the airfield, a reminder of the narrow country lanes which once criss-crossed the country. Along such lanes one could stroll before they were taken over by vehicles ever increasing in number and driven at faster and faster speeds. Now you would walk along them at your peril, particularly in the countryside. Ah, the blessing and the curse of the motor car. The impact of modern development on these tracks could be seen particularly clearly on the road to the north of the new village. Beyond it were wide tarmac roads, busy with cars, and lined with houses, but within the area of the former airfield the same 'roads' were green lanes along which for centuries people have taken their horses and carts, ridden or walked. Hazel hedges marked the bounds of these 'roads', overgrown and no longer laid as they would once have been. The tracks were a delight to discover, as were the fields and woods through which one could also walk. I loved finding the gentle impressions my predecessors had made on the landscape. Within the woodland there were straight hedge lines which once separated fields and old gateposts marked field entrances long unused. There was more to this area than was first apparent. And I could walk here? Yes, apparently one could ramble freely without anyone saying you had no right to be there. It was unbelievable. Sometimes the countryside is so busy and shut off that it feels an unfriendly place. Here one could wander at leisure and my wounds could heal. It was an unexpected time warp. The dogs and I began to explore these new places. Oddly, there were no rabbits, a few pheasants for Evie and a lot of foxes. Sadie was in her element.

It was November, just two weeks after I had moved in, and we were exploring the woods. The dogs were off their leads and my arm could now recover; Sadie was so bad on a lead, always resenting the restraint. Instantly she was off into the woods after foxes or fairies, who knew. The question was always the same, 'would she ever come back?' Soon there was no dog visible in the dense woodland and as daylight turned into the gloom of a late autumn afternoon she was nowhere to be seen. Stupidly I went off the track looking for her and found myself in the middle of scrub with no torch. I was totally lost. Back at the farm I would have known exactly where I was, on or off a track, but here I hadn't got a clue. Evie was close by me but of Sadie there was no sound. No yelping as she followed her prey, no rustle of leaves or breaking of twigs; total silence. I hate losing my way in woods. It is so easy to go round in circles as there is no point of reference. I confess I panicked and then suddenly, to my great relief, I found myself back on the track. Apart from my desperate shouts there was still the unwelcome silence and it was now pitch black. I walked back towards the start of the woods and heard a car slow down suddenly and a horn sound. It had to be Sadie. I ran to the road thinking she had been run over but there was no sign of her. Was she injured somewhere? I walked home fearing the worst, only to find her sitting on the doorstep. I was so pleased to see her and I think she was pleased to see me, but one was never sure with Sadie. She was probably thinking, 'where on earth have you been, it's dinner time.'

It was easy to take Evie for granted. She was such a loyal, obedient dog who never tested one's patience, always did what she was asked to do, and was just faultless. A friend of mine offered a home to Sadie should I die before her. 'I would love to have Sadie but I couldn't possibly have Evie, she is just too boring.' There's a lot to be said for a boring dog. How this woman would have got on with Sadie I can't imagine.

There was one very big problem with the new house and the walks we went on; there were far too many exciting things for Sadie to explore. The owner of some free range hens was unsurprisingly angry to find a dog with her head through the wire trying to get at his birds. Following my cries he returned her with the warning that if she tried to get in again she would be shot. Huge fields of rape offered acres for Sadie to explore and she took advantage of the opportunities. In she would dive, into jungles from which I never thought she would escape and then suddenly out she would fly at the same breakneck speed. The most dangerous time to be walking Sadie was at dusk for then a different world of animals emerged, more numerous and tempting than any of the daytime quarry. It was growing dark as we walked across the fields and Sadie suddenly put her nose into some long grass at the side of the path. There was a hissing and I thought it was a snake. I called Sadie away quickly and later spoke to the farmer who said it would have been a young barn owl. There was a colony of these birds nearby and that certainly did make sense. We had our second warning. 'The barn owls are protected so keep your dog away.' In fact the barn owls were protected only as long as it took a developer to cast his eye over the derelict buildings, buy them and turn the buildings into houses. What happened to the birds who had lived there I have no idea. I never saw them again.

Sadie hunted by sight while Evie used her spaniel's nose. Evie was one day tracking the scent of foxes methodically through a wood. I could see what she was after for in the distance three foxes were watching her. I assume they were deciding which direction they would have to run in when they suddenly had to made a quick decision. Sadie had arrived on the scene, seen the foxes and was off in hot pursuit, yelping excitedly. Evie joined in and they were both racing through the woods. Foxes and hounds crossed the path just in front of me and I waited to see what happened. The foxes outran the dogs, recrossed the path and ended up precisely where they had started. Clever animals are foxes. They had run the dogs in a circle and were obviously none the worse for the chase. The dogs, on the other hand, flopped down in front of me, totally exhausted.

Sadie's capacity for getting into trouble showed no signs of abating. Going away from home all would be as well as it ever was but turning towards home was the point at which she would decide to run off. Whether this was deliberate or not, it was very annoying. In the house she was even more annoying. Stairs were a new feature as we had lived in a bungalow. Coming down stairs Sadie would get hold of your feet and I was frightened to death she might pull me downstairs. First floor windows were another new feature which she had to get used to. Her instinct had always been to go through any open window and I grabbed her one day as she was half way through a bedroom window. That could have ended very badly. Impulsive was Sadie; lovable, impulsive, and very annoying.

My solution for settling into my new home was to walk. I felt like a refugee transplanted unwillingly to a new land and I walked and walked until the place felt a little more like home. This suited the dogs very well. Not that I ever tired Sadie out of course. We might get back from a day-long walk and she would be bouncing around saying, 'where are we going now.' She was your worst house guest. She also was still relatively young. When I moved, Sadie was four and Evie was two. One of the first people I met as I walked around commented on one of the dogs. 'What a lovely old dog,' she said. I thought she meant Sadie, but no, it was Evie she was referring to! Lovely, quiet, biddable Evie.

Letting Sadie off the lead had its usual problems. At the farm she could go across a field without restrictions, but here the distances between open space and houses was much smaller. I always (well, almost always) trusted that she would come back but didn't always know where she had been in the meantime. Sometimes one was all too aware and sometimes Evie and I walked on, fearing the worst. The two dogs were happily snuffling around in a coppice one day, when Sadie suddenly saw something out of the corner of her eye which was much more exciting - a cat. I called, but didn't want to highlight the fact that someone's cat was on the run, when a woman came out of one of the houses and beckoned me over. 'YOUR dog,' she said slowly and emphatically, 'has just chased MY cat into MY house, followed her in, eaten her food, and left.' I struggled not to laugh but the owner was definitely not laughing. On another occasion it wasn't cat food that Sadie stole. Out walking on a beautiful day she hopped through a gap in a fence, into someone's garden, and returned with half a pizza in her mouth. We walked swiftly and quietly on, fearing the all too familiar phrase, 'your dog…' I wondered how the missing pizza was explained. Dining al fresco had its risks with Sadie about.

Sadie's principle on food was simple. Anything which was in her reach was hers. This included food which was on a table for she happily leapt up to devour anything which was not closely guarded. She would even cheekily try to eat from the opposite side of a plate one was eating from. We had made no progress on this matter from that first night of trying to take the pie out of the oven. Generally there was no aggression involved, apart from the time she took a large joint of beef from the kitchen into the garden and was baring her teeth at anyone who dared to retrieve it. The joint was to feed four of us and it wasn't the time to be faint-hearted. Eventually the meat was restored to the kitchen. It had lost a little on its journey and some cosmetic modification was required, but there it was, safe, and almost sound. On the other hand one could see how she ended up in the Pound. Every day was an act of faith that she would behave in at least a half-decent way and not let me down. Most of the time that faith was misplaced.

One of Sadie's saving graces (and Evie's for that matter) was the way she adapted to her new circumstances. Bikes might race past her, runners, skate boards, nothing worried her. She never bounded at them as she might have. Mind you, on her travels through Montgomery unaccompanied, she had probably seen them all before but nonetheless it was a great bonus that when we were out walking I could trust that there was no aggression in either dog. Out walking with a friend and her dogs in some woods where there happened to be a cross-country race, I was shocked that her usually well-behaved dogs barked at every runner that went by. Cyclists apparently received the same treatment. I was beginning to feel that Sadie was not all bad. Evie, of course, one could guarantee would not deign to behave in such a way. Children adored Sadie because she looked so cute. You could guarantee that when they said, 'can I stroke your dog,' it was Sadie they were referring to and not Evie.

I was very anxious that Sadie might be missing something in her life, that walks alone might not be exciting enough. I wondered if dog agility might give her something to fill the gap which was left by having no sheep. What Sadie made of it I can only deduce from her behaviour. We gave it a good try over several weeks, but fences she would have leapt with ease in different circumstances she couldn't be bothered with. The tunnel seemed to give other dogs obvious pleasure but Sadie simply refused to go through. The trainer had a solution. If I scrambled through the tunnel first, Sadie would follow. Through the tunnel I went, only to find Sadie waiting for me at the other end, ready to lick my face and congratulate me on my achievement. I laughed but the trainers were not amused. By now they had had enough and glances in my direction indicated that it was time to leave. Psychologically I had taken several steps back.

We had been through a lot, the dogs and I. Sadie in particular had come a long way from her days of running off to become a valuable sheepdog and most of all a good friend. The move from the farm had not caused the dogs any trauma as far as I could tell and while I had yet to find a purpose in my life, it would happen eventually.

10

A LONG HOLIDAY

Someone shouted, 'There's a dog on the roof,' and Carole answered, 'That will be Sadie, she'll be fine.'

Now that I was settled it was time for a holiday and what else could it be but a walking holiday? The plan was that a friend, Carole, and I would spend four days walking part of the Coast to Coast Path from St Bees Head eastwards. Carole lived in the Lake District and had done the walk many times, while I was a novice and knew nothing about backpacking. I had bought a tent which I had been told would be suitable for the job in hand and I had a pair of newish walking boots which Sadie had kindly modified, eating half the tongue of one of them.

I had also got a new car and for the journey the dogs were to be kept in the boot area behind a dog grill. It took a while to fit the device but, with dogs and rucksack packed, off we went. It was May and the weather was set fair. We were all excited but Sadie was certainly not impressed with the travel arrangements and decided to modify them without delay. With head through the bars she plunged forwards demolishing the dog guard, and sat on the front seat with a look that said, 'that's better, now I'm in charge.' Sadie on the front seat wasn't easy. She moved around as though the seat was red hot until eventually she got tired and went to sleep. Evie's pose, meanwhile, was of resignation; she sat stock-still however long the journey.

It was early afternoon when I got to Ambleside and found my friend's cottage. I parked in the drive and got the dogs out. It had been a long drive of three and a half hours. To greet us was my friend's Hungarian Vizsla, a dog of impeccable manners. What he would make of Sadie I couldn't imagine. The dogs went through the house and into the back garden. I had Sadie on a lead but Carole said, 'you can let her off, Jane, she can't go anywhere.' Kettle on and I thought I had better check that Sadie was all right. There in the garden was Evie, but Sadie was nowhere to be found. I confess I panicked, as behind the fence was the road to the Kirkstone Pass, a busy road at any time of day. This was the trouble with Sadie, people underestimated her. Normal rules just didn't apply. It made me slightly worried about how we would get on in a tent. Would she hear something in the night and then suddenly fly through the side of the tent? The immediate problem was that she had disappeared. Where on earth could she be? I went to the front door to search for her and there she was waiting to come back in. She didn't like to be shut out, and she didn't like waiting, either. I breathed a very large sigh of relief. Our adventure could begin.

We walked into Ambleside to catch a bus to the train station and then we were to catch a train to St Bees. This was my first experience of carrying a very large backpack and it felt fine. As an added bonus the sun even shone. Sadie couldn't resist diving into a box of dog toys outside a pet shop and coming out with a squeaky toy, but there was no time for that; our bus awaited. Neither of my dogs had been on a bus and Sadie found the concept of sitting on the floor rather than on a seat like everyone else, totally incomprehensible. It was the same on the very crowded train. 'What a daft idea,' she seemed to say, 'if I can't get a seat as you have been lucky to do, at least let me sit on the table.' Hard work was Sadie! Not too soon it was St Bees Head but how on earth was I going to get off this train safely? Assuming I could get through the narrow door then how was I to make the descent to the platform which looked as though it was about three feet below me. Trains were designed for the orderly departure of one person at a time with, perhaps, a small case, not for someone with all my baggage. I was sure the rucksack would get stuck, and one or both of the dogs would end up on the railway line. Somehow we managed our departure from the train and ended up safely on the platform. St Bees Head is noted as the start of the Coast to Coast Walk and an area of outstanding natural beauty but for me it is the place where there is an insane drop from the train onto the platform.

And then we were off, walking to our first campsite. We arrived, pitched our tents against a fence, and settled down to our first night under canvas. After a good night's sleep, we set off on the first part of our journey. The sun shone, although it was crisp and windy. The dogs looked as though they were up for the challenge and we were away. St Bees Head was the customary stopping-off point for a photograph and then we headed inland. Down a quiet road I let the dogs off the lead and we met our first problem. No, not from Sadie, who was busy sniffing out rabbits in the hedgerow, but from Evie, who went through a gate and into a field of sheep. She refused to return and although the sheep weren't bothered by her presence, I could imagine a farmer shooting her. The ewes hadn't yet lambed and any trauma could be fatal to them or their offspring. I was panicking and then as I got to the gate I could see where Evie was and why she was there. The smell of a long-dead sheep wafted across the field, clearly irresistible to a spaniel's nose. Eventually Evie returned, perhaps the rotting carcass was too much even for her robust stomach.

We walked on and Sadie who had set off like a greyhound, soon realised that she had to match the pace of the steady Evie. We were in lowland Cumbria, walking through places which were a memory from my study of geography such as Cleator. On and on we went through marshes and conifer woods and into open moorland towards Ennerdale Bridge. The dogs trotted happily on, but I was definitely not trotting. My tent was giving me grief. It was heavy and bulky. I had trusted the man in the shop who said this would suit me perfectly. It might have been had I had a sherpa to carry it, but it was far too cumbersome for what I needed. Dogs curl up small. I could have got a pack of hounds into this one, and it refused to sit squarely on my back, leaning over to one side and pulling at my chest. By the end of the day I thought my aorta would burst, the pain was so great. Complaining would have added to my problems so I carried on, talking with Carole about nothing in particular. And this was how we came unstuck - taking our eye off the ball. Not far from our destination, we took the wrong path and had to backtrack about a mile to pick up the correct route. On a normal day this wouldn't have been a problem but with a rucksack containing enough dog food for four days and an oversize tent, this was not what I needed. Fortunately we were not far from our destination for the night, a pub at Ennerdale Bridge which had a campsite attached. The joy of seeing a group of houses in the distance, growing closer with each weary footstep, lifted our spirits. If I had been less tired I would have been excited. In we went, to find some devastating news.

The pub was under new ownership and the new landlord didn't allow camping. Carole had stayed there not long before so this was a bombshell. Knowing that the pub also had rooms to let, Carole asked if they were dog friendly. The landlord looked at the dogs lying exhausted under one of the tables and decided they were not. The locals told us that there was a campsite a mile up the road and Carole suggested that we got a taxi there. I had my doubts as to whether a taxi would miraculously appear in this remote village and whisk us to a better place. We still had choices and I was very definite. 'I'm having a beer.' I sat down with the dogs fast asleep in front of a roaring fire while Carole tried to appeal to the landlord's better nature to allow us to camp on the land adjacent to the pub. Anyone could see it was hopeless but some of the locals joined in for this was the most excitement they had had for a while. Unfortunately, their judgment was flawed by a certain haziness in their brains and they failed to notice that the more they remonstrated the more the landlord was determined we weren't going to stay. With apologies for the mixed metaphors; lines were drawn, the barricades were up, and the landlord held all the ace cards. Just as we had run out of options, except another beer (perhaps this is what happened to the locals, they just ran out of options), one of the men, older than the others, quietly came over and suggested a solution. Adjacent to his house he had a piece of land on which we were welcome to pitch our tents for the night. Carole was still hitting her head against the brick wall of the landlord when I tapped her on the shoulder and told her of the offer. We were so grateful. The land was literally just around the corner from the pub. We pitched our tents and returned for our evening meal.

On our return our earlier plight seemed to have stuck in the minds of two of the men but its resolution seemed to have passed them by. One would come over and ask, 'have you found anywhere to stay yet?' A little while later the other would ask the same question. Suddenly one of them came over and told us this story about his childhood. 'When I was a child my family was very poor and we had no bath in the house except for a tin bath which for most of the week hung on a cherry tree in the garden. Every Sunday the bath was taken into the house and put in front of the fire. It was then filled with hot water which turned brown from the rust and each member of the family from the oldest to the youngest would have a bath. As the youngest member I sometimes thought I came out of the bath dirtier than when I went in. Once our washing was over, the bath was hung back up on the cherry tree and became a pirate ship which I sailed in the beck at the bottom of the garden. I could do what I wanted with the bath during the week as long as it was back on its hook by Sunday.' It was a sweet story and we laughed politely but in truth it fell rather flat. Perhaps the beer had taken something away from the narrative or perhaps I was just too tired to care.

Along the way other people told us their stories. We met a farmer on a track and with Sadie ahead of us I was nervous when his van slowed down and he poked his head out of the window, even more so when he got out of his van. I was sure I would be told off for having the dog off the lead but, no, he simply wanted to talk, to pass the time of day, and tell us a little of his story. Now in his seventies he had moved back to the Lakes after working in Basildon. He bought a farm and no sooner had the mortgage been paid than his wife died. His son constantly questioned why his father still spent so many hours working. He tried to explain to him that it wasn't work but pleasure. I understood and envied his lifestyle.

Bistro food was how the landlord had described the pub fare, whatever that meant. In reality it was frozen food badly reheated. The result was certainly one of the worst meals I have ever eaten. As we were finishing our meal, the sandwiches put up for the walkers the next day were being brought out of the kitchen. That would nicely warm up the bacteria I thought. Carole suggested we should order some sandwiches as there was nowhere to eat on our walk the next day. I asked if mine could be left in the fridge overnight but doubted they would be.

The next day we were to walk from Ennerdale Bridge to Rosthwaite via Black Sail but it had rained all night and when we woke it was still pouring. We packed up the tents, the rain having made my already heavy tent even heavier, and we started our walk in torrential rain. Huge raindrops were falling, and Carole decided that we should take the valley route along the side of Ennerdale.

This would be a nice walk on a dry day but it was still raining hard so that every step had to be taken with care. Stony slopes and narrow gullies could spell disaster. Going up and coming down were terrifying and I wanted to say that I couldn't do it, but there was no choice. Eventually the path evened out, but just before it did there was a torrent and crossing it was slippery. I lost my footing and ended up with water in my boot. Even with Sadie's modification of the tongue, the boots were not high enough up my ankle for this sort of walking. I stopped to change my sock and then we carried on across the end of Ennerdale and on to a forest track to take us up to Black Sail, my wet boot chafing my foot with every step. On the plus side, the rain had stopped and a stiff breeze had got up. Blowing from behind us we were making good time but when we arrived at Black Sail the wind was no longer a blessing but a curse of gale force proportions. It was clear that we would be going no further that day but there was a problem about staying where we were. No camping was allowed in the area of the youth hostel and no dogs were allowed in it. No-one could leave their dogs out in this weather all night and it was too dangerous for us to go further. For now there was only one thing to do; to have a cup of tea and wait for the warden of the hostel to arrive. The dogs, much against Sadie's wishes, stayed firmly outside. Evie and the Vizsla curled up in hollows, protected against the elements, but Sadie took a different tack. With the door and the windows all firmly shut she got up on the roof to see if there was a secret entrance there. One of the other guests, fearing she may be stuck, suddenly came running in shouting, 'there's a dog on the roof.' Neither Carole nor I moved and it was Carole who spoke, without concern, 'that'll be Sadie, she'll be fine.' And she was fine, of course, although there was no secret entrance and she was forced to snuggle up in her own hollow out of the wind.

The night was eventful to say the least. The gale increased to storm force and we managed to get an agreement from the warden that when everyone had gone to bed we could all sleep in the Youth Hostel on condition that the dogs would be outside the following morning before everyone woke. It was a sensible solution but I was naive enough to think we could still sleep in the tents. Carole's tent went up perfectly. Mine, on the other hand, succumbed to the force of the wind and there was a tremendous crack as one of the tent poles broke. We did stay in the tents, but only for half the night. It was too dangerous to be outside and the dogs realised it; they just couldn't settle. We spent the rest of the night safe and warm in the Hostel.

In the morning we resumed our walk in dry weather although the ground underfoot was sodden with the rain of the previous days. Paths had become streams and streams had become rivers, with stepping stones deep below the surface of the water. The fast flowing water threatened to whisk you off your feet as you felt for the stones with your walking pole. Without the floods my clumsy backpack meant such crossings had to be made cautiously, but it was Evie who nearly met her Maker.

One minute she was sitting on a rock above a ravine, and the next minute her leg slipped and she nearly fell to a certain death. Somehow she managed to regain her balance and scramble off. Carole saw this and was characteristically calm. 'I'm glad you didn't see that, Jane.' I, too, was glad I hadn't seen it. We walked down to our campsite - the one we should have stayed at the night before. It had been a short day but we needed it, well, I needed it, anyway. With our tents pitched once more, the sun shone for the first time since we left St Bees, and the dogs stretched out, exhausted.

The next day we walked the short distance into Grasmere and then caught the bus back to Ambleside. Our adventure was over. We were going home.

11

Finding four hundred photographs of India from the early part of the twentieth century seemed like a wonderful opportunity

MY TURN

It was my turn now to find a purpose in life. Losing the farm had left a big hole that for me was not going to be filled by walking, holidays or coffee mornings. I have always taken pleasure in work and holidays simply aren't my thing. I had time to fill and decided, at the age of 62, to try something new.

Sorting through ephemera from the farm I found about four hundred photographs of India at the beginning of the twentieth century. Perhaps if I hadn't found them I could have saved myself a lot of time and trouble. However I did find them and thought that as the photographs were part of Indian history rather than mine, the internet was the perfect place to share them. There was just one problem. There was no obvious place to put them. I reasoned that other people must have the same problem so I would create a place online where people could share their history. The result would be that the jigsaw of the past would acquire some extra pieces and therefore could be more clearly understood. I set myself a budget and sought a designer who could do the job of creating the site. Simple, or so I thought.

While I was asking for something complex, there was nothing that hadn't been done elsewhere, but had I known that it would take nearly two years to complete, and ten years later I would still be wrestling with getting the site I wanted, I might have thought twice about embarking on this venture. Finding the right person to do the job was essential, but it was like looking for a needle in a haystack. Any online search of web designers threw up a large number of results, but how was I to choose one rather than another? How was I to sift out those who could do the job from those who couldn't, and those who were going to give value for money from those who were definitely not to be trusted? I fumbled my way from one potential web designer to another trying not to repeat a previous mistake only to make a different one the next time.

In the end I have to admit that the choice I made was not my finest. I shared my idea in the hope that the web designer, Mike, and I would work together but as soon as the contract had been signed and the first instalment of money handed over, we appeared to go our separate ways. To be specific, Mike seemed to have gone his own way and was now completely incommunicado. Emails and phone calls were met with total silence and in this day and age of constant availability, silence is a powerful message. The work meanwhile had been delegated to two people, a freelancer who would put the ideas into practice while I was, by default, in charge of quality control. That left me with a heavy workload because so much didn't work. Completion was due in five weeks but the deadline came and went without so much as an acknowledgment from Mike. The excitement I had had at the start was long gone and replaced by deep concern. The only thing one could depend on arriving on time were the invoices. On the due date a bill would appear indicating that payment was expected. The dilemma was that the work had been done but not, as far as I was concerned, to the required standard. Was I therefore entitled to withhold payment? I simply didn't know and was powerless and frightened to refuse. This was as far from the partnership of equality and mutual trust I had hoped for as it was possible to be. I was merely a pawn in this game and I had no idea where or how it would end. The effort of this daily impasse took its toll and I was coming to the unpleasant conclusion that my hopes were never going to be realised when suddenly, quite out of the blue, several months after the job should have been finished, the web designer rang and asked if he could visit to explain his silence. Sadie was excited to see anyone but as he bent down to stroke her she jumped up and bit him on the nose. Retribution was delivered in one nip; what a clever dog. After another month's hard work even I had to admit that the final result was just not good enough. Sometimes one has to admit that abandoning ship is the only solution. It had been an expensive lesson.

Sensible people would have given up at this stage but another web designer approached me with an offer to help me get my money back from Mike's company. Believing that my money was by now long gone, I gave my knight in shining armour (well, the armour shone at that moment although in time it lost its sheen) and his company the job of creating the website. They put the nuts and bolts together and made something that worked. It wasn't as pretty as I would have liked nor as functional, but with the budget spent, I wasn't going to spend any more.

Because there was room for improvement I looked for extra funding only to find more blind alleys. It was always, 'if only.' 'If only you had been an artist,' 'if only it hadn't been digital,' 'if only it was family history and not all history.' And then suddenly there seemed to be the opportunity I had been waiting for. I was invited to apply to join a development programme for new online businesses. The man in charge of the programme spoke of my business being a perfect fit and the selection interview sounded like a formality. 'Don't worry,' he said, 'leave all your questions until you are on the programme then you will get technical, marketing and business support.' Not wishing to leave anything to chance I worked for two months honing my presentation.

I imagined that I would be presenting my ideas to a panel of interviewers sitting behind a desk, so was surprised to be taken into a tiny room in which a number of men sat tightly packed in a chaotic group. I sidled in and sat on the one spare chair. I gave my presentation and the head of the programme was the first to speak. 'That is amazing, Jane. You tick all the boxes. You use all the right buzz words.' I detected a sting in this insect's tail. There was silence. To my right a man was looking at his laptop and shared something with the man sitting next to him. I began to feel uneasy. This wasn't going well. On my left a man asked, 'what is your revenue stream?' I had suggested that this would become evident as the website was developed during the programme. My inadequate answer was just what the man needed to launch his attack. It was his moment and he didn't waste it. 'I don't know how you are going to make money out of this. It reminds me of the underpants gnomes in South Park where their profit strategy is to first collect underpants.' Everyone in the room laughed heartily, everyone except me, of course. I hadn't got a clue what he was talking about. Unknown to me this was an in-joke amongst the IT fraternity when there is a website which has been set up with no integral way of making money. I was not expected to reply; the interview was at an end. I had worked for two months for an interview of less than ten minutes and been utterly humiliated. I managed to walk out of the building with my head held high before the floodgates holding back my composure opened and my heart broke.

The psychological kneecapping I had received was devastating and took me to depths of depression far deeper than leaving the farm because this was a black hole of my own making. Despair followed me everywhere I went and tainted even that most pleasurable experience, walking the dogs. It was hard to regain any sense of self worth after the underpants experience. I remember an artist telling me about her humiliating experience concerning an exhibition in which her art had featured. Visitors had said a lot of nice things about her paintings, and she was quietly pleased with the day. Returning home on the underground, the train was strewn with newspapers. She picked up a copy, and there, as she knew it would be, was a review of the exhibition. There was even a very nice image of one of her paintings, but underneath, to her horror, was a scathing review of her work. She wanted to cry, to walk along the train and collect every newspaper so that no-one should read the article, but most of all she wanted to hide; her shame was more than she could bear. For the first time in her life she realised how vulnerable her creativity had made her and over the forthcoming weeks and months she questioned whether it was worth it. The pure pleasure in working was replaced by a hitherto unknown self consciousness and diffidence. Depression and panic attacks became an unwelcome accompaniment to everyday life.

The artist, thankfully, didn't give up painting nor did I give up on the website. I emailed another web designer and after a couple of business-like emails to and fro he gave his opinion of the website. After a scathing review he concluded. 'Have I made you cry yet?' Those closest to us pick up the pieces after such experiences and put us back together as well as they can but the scars remain. In my case it was left to Sadie and Evie to bring me out of my despair. Evie smothered me with love and Sadie reminded me that I had better sort myself out for there were walks to be done.

It was clear that IT was not where my future lay. I looked around for other options but the fact was that I had lost confidence in myself. After months of more blind alleys I was at rock bottom when one Saturday morning I decided to visit a local man who I knew was very knowledgeable about the history of the area. I had been too shy to speak to him before but now I felt that I had nothing to lose. I knocked on the door of his cottage and nervously explained that I was studying the history of the parish. 'What do you want to know?' He asked. 'I want to know what you know,' I said. I thought it was rather cheeky of me but the truth was I hadn't got a clue how to answer the question. Frank chuckled and invited me in. With none of the usual preliminaries, he walked over to a glass cabinet and took out a small object which he put into my hand. It was a tiny black and coloured ornament in the shape of a duck which was, he explained, an enamelled Roman brooch. I was taken aback by the history in my hands and this mark of trust. Perhaps Frank now wanted to see how serious I was, for the conversation was at an end for that day. 'Come back next Saturday,' he said, 'and I will show you some more.' To my surprise, the following Saturday he whisked me off at great speed to a local farm. Frank was a man of extreme contrasts, driving as though there wasn't a moment to lose and walking slowly across fields with his metal detector taking care to miss nothing as he went. Inside the farmhouse was a glass case with artefacts. I had never seen anything like this except in a museum, and the thought that each object had been found locally gave a connection with the past I had not felt before. There was a lot to learn and I had found the best teacher I could possibly have had.

Frank was born into a family of tenant farmers on the Shropshire Hills where making ends meet was a constant struggle. Although Frank went to the local grammar school, his parents couldn't afford to send him to university and he became a farm labourer. He applied his prodigious intelligence to the study of wild flowers and wild life of all sorts. Always a great reader and book collector, he then added bottle collecting, and finally metal detecting to his interests. Frank's wife, Mary, shared her husband's interests in every respect apart from formal education, having preferred not to go to school at all. 'I hated school,' she said, 'my father used to take me so far on his bike and then go home but I was always back home before him!' One could understand the temptation, the confines of a classroom versus the open spaces of the Shropshire Hills. I, too, remember my primary school education. While I didn't hate school, the highlight of the day was the walk back home, a group of us, across the fields. Not least it gave me a love of wild flowers which still give me enormous pleasure.

Every Saturday over the weeks that followed, Frank showed me a variety of artefacts such as flints, clothes fastenings, coins of all sorts, decorative pendants for bridles, brooches, buttons and sheep bells. Each told their part of history in a vivid way and I knew I was both privileged to see the collection and to be trusted not to divulge more than I should. We were about a month into my education when Frank suddenly said, 'there could be a book in this.' I confess I thought, 'oh, no, I have more than enough to do,' but it was the least I could do to repay Frank's generosity. I had the partnership I was looking for, and it had come from a totally unexpected direction, just three miles from where I live now and where I had lived at the farm. Frank, too, felt that he had found someone he could work with. One day he said, 'I've waited for 30 years to find someone to share this information with.' What a strange world that I was that person and what was it about me that was different? Was it simply that I took the time to listen? I knew that Frank was ill and there was no time to lose in writing the book. I was in learning mode once again because I didn't know how to put a book together but we did it and we were a good team. All too soon Frank died but my friend and mentor had left me a priceless legacy. We had shared similar values and developed a deep friendship. We understood each other, it was as simple as that. The legacy went further. Frank had a sister who was part of a group translating documents from Medieval Latin. I joined this group and painfully added another dimension to my exploration of local history. I am still working with Frank's sister and two others from the group ten years later. I was back with those I understood and somehow I had found my place in the world.

The dogs were particularly pleased that I had recovered, for long walks could be enjoyed once more, and Sadie's cheeky behaviour could make me laugh again. If I told the dogs to stay in the house you could guarantee that Evie would stay and Sadie would sneak around my back as I went out of the door. I would put the key in the lock, look down and there she was looking up at me. Stay was a word she never quite 'got.' She could manage it for a short while, a very short while, but then she was off. I was visiting a nearby village and put Sadie and Evie to sit, while I turned away to look at the landscape. My back was turned for a moment and when I looked round she had gone. Evie, of course, was still sitting where she had been put and although I called, Sadie just didn't return. There were likely to be hens around and I envisaged her getting in and destroying them. It was all too quiet and then a friend walked over a field and heard her barking. Sadie had been going into or out of a wood when her collar got caught on a barbed wire fence. Thank goodness she had the sense to bark or that could have been the end of her.

What had caught Sadie's eye on that occasion I don't know, perhaps any minute she had to wait was a minute of her life which she considered wasted, but the reason for Sadie's detours on our local walks was usually associated with food and there were opportunities in abundance. People sat on benches enjoying a takeaway often with the food at their side. Sadie would spot her chance and slide the food onto the floor. If the diners were lucky either they or I would see the food being moved from underneath, if not, then it was Sadie's prize. I was beckoned over one day by a teenager who told me 'Your dog has just eaten my burger and chips.' Local people learnt to hold on to their food.

In one of the places where we walked, a piece of ground had been set aside for picnics and fenced off so that dogs would be excluded. I had never seen anyone use this area so I was surprised one day to see two young women and their children sitting on the ground tucking into a picnic laid out on a rug in front of them. 'That's dangerous,' I thought, and no sooner had I thought this than Sadie was heading straight for the food. The children jumped up, terrified by this intruder, and one of the women was very angry. 'That dog shouldn't be in here, get it out,' she shrieked. As I collected Sadie, without any food being lost, I might add, I pointed out that the dog wouldn't have been in there had the gate been shut. The whys and wherefores weren't the young woman's concern at this moment as much as staying on her high horse and adding a final comment to her friend as we departed, 'and that dog doesn't even look clean to me.' Poor Sadie (not that I often said that), did the woman think this should have been a black and white collie?

Car parks were one of Sadie's favourite foraging haunts. Sometimes she would be gone for so long that I thought she had been picked up as a stray. This happened from time to time and was a nuisance because I knew she would return sooner or later. On this occasion it was a Sunday morning and the car park was full of people going to church. A bag of chips had been left in the corner of the car park and Sadie took the shortest route through the legs of an elderly man who was standing near a car. Perhaps Sadie recognised the man for she then stopped and turned towards him. Unsurprisingly the poor man stumbled and put his hand out to steady himself against the car but worse was to come. At that moment the driver, not seeing the man's fingers in this vulnerable position, slammed the car door. When I met the man later at church his hand was heavily bandaged and as he told me the story he laughed at Sadie's naughtiness. He might have been as angry as the woman in the picnic area and with some justification but he wasn't and fortunately there was no permanent damage done.

12

AND FINALLY

One of our favourite walks was along the local canal

When I had moved to our new home Sadie was four years old. Five years then passed in which we shared many adventures. Every day was an adventure for Sadie although sharing is not quite the right word; most of the time Evie and I were at best onlookers and at worst simply hung around waiting around for Sadie's current adventure to end. My role was to provide the scenery, to decide where the dramas were to take place and to mitigate the impact of them when they threatened to get out of hand.

The two dogs continued to be great friends but when they were out on their walks they did their own thing and when Sadie ran off Evie would simply sit down and wait for her return. I might go looking for her, but Evie was resolute that she wouldn't do that. 'I'll just sit here and wait for Sadie to come back,' was the clear message. Every day, morning and afternoon we walked, afternoon walks taking place strictly at 3.00pm. If I was five minutes late, Sadie would give me a nudge, until one day there was no nudge and it was clear that she was not well. I phoned the vet and after an examination it was arranged that tests would be done. Two days later I had to ring and say that Sadie was much worse and I feared that she would have to be put down. And so it was that I lost my friend who had carried me from the farm and seen me through some dark times.

It goes without saying that other dog owners noted the gap immediately. Few words were spoken, they weren't necessary. What had happened was clearly visible in my face and this was not the time to answer any questions. Other dog owners know this sadness only too well. Everyone knew Sadie and everyone is shocked because it has happened so suddenly. I was shocked, too, partly because Sadie wasn't a particularly old dog and partly because her death had been so unexpected; there had been so little time to adjust. Anyone who has had a pet knows the depth of this grief. When you make the decision to have a dog you know in your head that you will only have your friend for a short while but when you lose them it is your heart and not your head that is in charge and your heart is broken.

Which brings me back to the beginning again. Some people never get over the grief of losing their best friend but Sadie had been special and let's face it, most of the time she had been especially difficult! Sadie had been put down on the Friday and I was due to go away on holiday on the Monday afterwards. I toyed with the idea of not going at all because I couldn't imagine that it would be enjoyable; it certainly wasn't going to be fun but staying at home wouldn't be fun either. The gap in my life would be painful wherever I was. In the end I went on holiday but came back a day early and sat down to write a piece about a particular week in Sadie's life. I don't like humanising animals but she just made you do that. I thought perhaps the last words should belong to Sadie so here is her diary for a typical week in her eventful life.

Saturday July 24

I have spent the morning helping my mistress tidy the garden. I am a great help, digging holes to put plants in, pruning back excessive growth, and general landscaping. I have made enormous changes in the garden and sometimes I don't think I am appreciated. In my opinion my mistress has what they call "a short fuse" far too often. She needs to relax and leave me to do more of the work. Anyway I had enormous fun chasing this frog through the undergrowth (which my mistress calls her flower border). The garden looked a lot tidier when I had finished, much flatter. My mistress shouted at me, as I say, I am just not appreciated. She even used the "n" word. 'You are a very naughty dog.' 'Words, words, are best ignored,' is my motto, so I wait until my mistress isn't looking and just carry on chasing whatever I can.

Sunday July 25

I have to say that our walks have been a little repetitive of late. I know my mistress has been rather busy but after all she has a responsibility to Evie and myself, as I sometimes have to remind her. We are walking late in the evening by a lake when I suddenly see a nice big fox hiding in the rushes. He thinks I can't see him, but even if I couldn't see him I would smell him. I fly into the reeds and grab hold of him but he runs off, leaving me with a mouthful of stinking fox hair. I was as close as I have ever been to catching a fox but the hair got the better of me. I return to my mistress still spitting out Reynard's hair only to be told off once again. 'Sadie, leave the foxes alone, you'll get bitten you stupid dog.' Moi, stupid, I think not. Next time.

Monday July 26

I meet a man with a large black and white dog. The dog isn't very friendly and the man isn't either and keeps his dog firmly on a lead so that it can't speak to me. Actually, I'm not particularly interested in speaking to it either but I know the man has some treats in his pocket and if I sit nicely he will let me have one. But what's this I see? Never mind the treats, he has a chicken hanging from his belt. That could be even better. I jump at it and put a slit in its side but to my disappointment it's not a real chicken but a toy. One squeak and it was officially dead. It wasn't my fault that the toy was made so badly that a little nip destroyed it but the man is very cross. My mistress apologises which I don't think she should have. It's a very odd thing to wear a chicken; asking for trouble if you would like my opinion.

Tuesday July 27

It's a hot day and we are strolling down a little lane when I hear a bird singing the other side of a hedge. Birds aren't really my 'thing,' I normally leave them to Evie, but she doesn't seem particularly interested. To my surprise, this bird can't fly away as it is in a cage and if I can just get my paws through the bars this will be a nice snack to keep me going. I try and try, but just can't quite catch it and in so doing the cage rattles and my mistress, who has been in a world of her own, suddenly realises what I am doing. There are calls one can ignore and calls one can't and this was of the latter kind - rather rude I thought and I am sure she used a very rude word when she referred to me as a little b….. Not nice. She was probably right though, I was wasting my time.

Wednesday July 28

We are going to visit a friend of my mistress and have a nice little walk through the woods. I take a small detour, of course, but wasn't away too long. It's another hot day and apart from squirrels there's not much about. I've done with chasing squirrels. I caught one once and it was disgusting. I put it down as soon as I could. I itched quite a lot afterwards and I didn't like those yellow teeth either. Anyway when we arrive at the friend's house, the side gate is opened and Evie and I are ushered into the garden. It hardly seems right that we dogs should be excluded from a house where biscuits will accompany a cup of tea, but this woman doesn't seem to like me. I have no idea what I have done to her but I get the distinct impression that Evie would be welcome in the house if I wasn't with her. That leaves me to find something to do in the garden. Evie is happy to lie down and take her ease, but that is not my way. Ah, ha, there is a nice pond in the garden. I wonder what is in there. A tasty fish would suit very well, so I begin to explore. Weed has to be taken out of the way and quite a lot of water goes down my throat but no fish. I am beginning to get bored when suddenly my mistress calls and I rush in, barging past Evie (she's far too slow, that one). Unfortunately all the water I have swallowed catches up with me and whoops, it lands on the new white carpet in the sitting room. The friend is furious. She doesn't say a lot but her lips are suddenly tight. She cleans the carpet as well as she can but I can't help noticing that there is still a greenish tinge to it. My mistress gathers Evie and myself up quickly and we go back home. My mistress is crying. I bet she wishes she hadn't come.

Thursday July 29

Fish are very nice if they are fresh and one of my favourite walks is along the canal. If my mistress is in a good mood we can walk nearly all day and meet hardly anyone. This day is different, all along the canal are people holding long sticks over the water. I'm in luck, dangling from one of the sticks is a fish and if I'm quick I can grab it before the man does, but no, I must be slowing down because I leap up but the man's hand is there before me. He looks at me and laughs and my mistress apologises and on we go.

Evie's favourite thing are pheasants but I can't be doing with all those feathers. They make me cough and get in my throat. Don't get me wrong, if one happens to cross my path I will chase it, so imagine my surprise when we are climbing up a steep hill one day and turn a corner to see that the path in front of us is covered with pheasants. Evie and I are off like rockets to clear the way but my mistress doesn't understand our interpretation of the situation and shouts at us to stop. Evie stops but I carry on until all the birds are in the air. Good job done, I think, but my mistress doesn't seem to agree.

Friday July 30

I hated leaving the farm but there's no doubt we have had some good walks since we left. A regular one is up quite a steep hill. When my mistress says we're going up the Wrekin I get even more excited than normal. On this particular day we call and pick up two friends, a woman and a black Labrador. Up the hill we go and, of course, I am first to the top. Our usual path takes us up over the top and down the other side so I lead the way. But where is my mistress? Surely she can't have gone ahead of me? I am lost, of that there is no doubt, and I am beginning to get very worried. I go back to the top of the hill but she isn't there. After a long time I hear my mistress's voice calling me but I am too frightened to move. A crowd has gathered, trying to coax me down, but I'm not going with them, they might try and steal me and I could end up even worse off than I am now. Wait, I think I can see my mistress in the distance, but I still can't be sure so I'll stay where I am. And then suddenly she is here by my side and everything is as it should be. 'Oh, Sadie,' she says, 'You are silly, I was right at the bottom when I realised you were missing. Why didn't you come when I called?' I'm a tough little dog so I don't like to admit that I was too frightened to move but I'm glad she found me. 'Come on, little one,' she says, and down we go.

It would have been lovely to have had Sadie for many more years but, as my daughter pointed out, she wasn't meant to slow down. An old, infirm, Sadie was impossible to imagine, so perhaps it was right that she died when she was still a very active dog. Evie lived happily on her own for another five years without having to share her mistress, and more importantly her sofa, with anyone else. And after Evie died was there another dog? Of course there was. A local Dog Rehoming Centre supplied me with a lovely Working Cocker Spaniel which they had found difficult to re-home. They thought we would make a good team and so we do.

ILLUSTRATIONS

Because the size of the book is small, the illustrations which are landscape can't be seen to their full effect, hence this section so that you can see them more clearly.

Fun loving free spirit seeks opportunity to hunt foxes, rabbits or squirrels. Happy to work as a sheepdog in return

Sadie moving the sheep far too fast!

Sadie off on her travels. The pure pleasure of being free.

Parts of the wood were very steep and it was here
that I would hide behind a tree and wait for Sadie to
run past so that I could grab her.

Nowadays big bales have almost totally
replaced small bales such as these and the hard
work of lugging and stacking small bales is fast
becoming a thing of the past.

Sadie was no threat to the lambs except that she would share their food.

The dogs were chalk and cheese; the obedient Evie on the left and the very disobedient Sadie. They both appear to be paying attention but something very different was going on in their heads.

With the pace of life today the beauty which is
around us can so easily be missed.

A typical farm dispersal sale.

You could almost hear the carts trundling along the lanes.

Sadie stages a rooftop protest.

Old photographs of India were the inspiration for a website.

One of our favourite walks along the canal took us past this lovely old bridge.

ABOUT THE AUTHOR

Jane Smith was born in Wolverhampton and has lived nearby for most of her life. Educated at Wolverhampton Girls' High School, she then went to Aberystwyth University where she studied Geography, and afterwards to Bradford University taking a further degree in Marketing. After various jobs in industry she then, with her husband, ran the small Shropshire farm featured in the book.

Printed in Poland
by Amazon Fulfillment
Poland Sp. z o.o., Wrocław

54754488R00073